Caught with Bibles

Caught With Bibles

A True Story from Communist Romania

Genovieva Sfatcu Beattie
with Stephen Beattie

VMI PUBLISHERS • SISTERS, OREGON

Published by
VMI Publishers
Sisters, Oregon
www.vmipublishers.com

All Scripture references are taken from the *Holy Bible, New International Version*. Copyright © 1973, 1978, 1984 International Bible Society. Used by permission of Zondervan Bible Publishers.

ISBN: 978-1-933204-81-9
ISBN: 1-933204-81-8

Library of Congress: 2008943814

Printed in the USA

Cover design by Juanita Dix

Note: Some of the names in this book have been changed.

CONTENTS

ACKNOWLEDGMENTS

As a correspondence student with the Institute of Children's Literature and Long Ridge Writers Group, West Redding, Connecticut, between 1994 and 1999, I should like to thank my wonderful instructors, Jean Soule, Ethel Paquin, Venita Helton, Patricia Pfitsch, and Kristi Holl, who taught me to write and helped me to break into print.

My special thanks go also to my husband, Stephen, who encouraged me to go on as I recalled the sad experiences from my life. He made many valuable suggestions and helped me at every stage, from typing the first draft to preparing the final manuscript for the publisher.

Genovieva Sfatcu Beattie

Chapter One

The Prophecy

A s the Lord brought Esther to royal position for such a time as this, so we in the free world have the call to rescue Christians behind the Iron Curtain," I concluded. Then I went to sit down at the back with my friends.

It was April 1985 and I was on a speaking trip in Switzerland. I had just given my testimony in a church, which met in an old stone building. There were long wooden benches and an aisle down the middle. The church had a balcony at the back. In the front, on the communion table, was a vase of daffodils. There was singing with clapping of hands, accompanied by drums, guitars and a piano. The atmosphere in the meeting that evening was wonderful. I was amazed that so many people of all ages were there on a weeknight.

"Our pastor receives prophetic words for people," my friend Linda explained.

"That's why hundreds flock to hear him," her husband, Henry, added.

I wanted to hear a word from the Lord myself, but not the one I was about to get.…

The pastor was a tall man in his late forties. At the end of the meeting he gave several specific prophecies for people in the congregation. One of them seemed to be for me.

"The Lord shows me a young woman dressed in black," he started. "He says that tomorrow morning you will receive bad news in the mail.… Satan will try to destroy you through this news. But the Lord says to be strong and to remember the story of Job. The Lord will bring good out of it in the end. This is the sign that this prophetic word is from the Lord: You have a pain in your back on the right, but when you get home the pain will go. Here is a Scripture to encourage you: 'We know that in all things God works for the good of those who love him'" (Romans 8:28).

I am wearing a black velvet dress, I thought. *I also have a pain in my back as he described, and I didn't tell anyone about it.* Still, I hoped that this prophetic word was not for me.

After the service was over, I stood at the door with the pastor and shook hands with everyone. Then I went home with my Swiss friends. When we arrived at their apartment we had a cup of hot chocolate, and I went to bed for the night. I drew the bedroom curtains to see the moon and stars through the window. I thanked the Lord for the day and lay down to sleep under the soft quilt. Then I realized that the pain in my back had gone....

The next morning my hosts prepared breakfast. We had coffee with boiled milk, the way I liked it. We ate freshly baked rolls with homemade raspberry jam. From the breakfast table, through the large window, I could see the sunrise. I looked at the swans on the nearby lake and enjoyed the beauty and calm.

At that moment the door bell rang. Linda got up and went to the door. It was the mail carrier.

"Genovieva," she said when she returned, "there is a telegram for you from Romania."

For eighteen years, my family had been involved in the distribution of Bibles, and the Lord had protected us in this work. Last night's prophecy filled me with a renewed sense of foreboding.

I quickly read the telegram. It was from my brother, Teodor. It said in coded language, "Constantin was caught with Bibles. All the family is in trouble." Constantin, or Costică as we called him, was another of my brothers in Romania.

I was devastated and cried for a long time. Linda and Henry tried to comfort me, but in vain. I went to my room and knelt down by my bed. The pain I felt was deep and would not go away. To be caught with Bibles in Romania was a crime, and Romanian prisons were like Nazi death camps.

I asked the Lord to tell me what to do. Suddenly I knew I had to go to Austria to talk to Stephen. We had arranged this shipment of Bibles together.

———————————

In a residential district of Vienna, Stephen was at his office desk. He worked with a mission that smuggled Bibles into Eastern Europe. He took many trips a year into the different communist countries, including Romania.

Stephen was from England and his job at this time was to send out teams of young people into the East with Bibles. It was dangerous work, especially when vehicles were detained at the borders and their cargo confiscated. Although the mission operated from a free country, the whole team always had to be secretive, because there were communist spies around, even in Austria. Stephen kept the trip reports in order and the correspondence with other missions up to date.

The phone rang.

"Genovieva, is that you?" he said. "What? Caught with Bibles?" He closed his eyes as his friend explained about the telegram she'd received, and dread washed over him. "Yes, come as soon as possible. I will arrange a place for you to stay.… We will pray for them and publicize the situation."

———————————

The next day I set out for Austria. After a day's drive, I arrived in Vienna. The mission office was a two-story house on a quiet road. In the front was a cherry tree in blossom. I walked up the steps and rang the bell. Stephen opened the door and welcomed me. I followed him into the living room, where we sat down in armchairs around a little table. Some of the young people gathered in his house were memorizing addresses for their next trip. They looked up as if they expected me.

"What exactly happened?" Stephen asked. In his early thirties, with dark hair and hazel eyes, he radiated passion for our cause. "As far as we know, all the Bibles and children's books were safely distributed. It was a miracle how quickly all your children's books went in."

"Yes, that's true," I said. "It was the very last load of six hundred Bibles and some children's books that was caught."

It felt so good to be able to share my burden with Stephen and the team. One of the girls, Becky, brought a tray of coffee and cakes.

"How did you get out of Romania, Genovieva?" she asked.

"The Lord rescued me as He rescued Daniel from the lion's den," I said. "President Jimmy Carter intervened to get me out of Romania. Soon after I arrived in America in March 1980, I visited Washington DC. There a lady at the State Department showed me my name mentioned twice in reports by the Helsinki Commission for Human Rights. That is how I received the best visa to come to the United States—that of a political refugee."

"How did you come to write the beautiful children's books we took into Romania?" Stephen asked.

"When I arrived in the United States, one of the places that fascinated me the most was Christian bookstores. There was nothing like that in Romania. I gazed for hours at cards with beautiful pictures and Bible verses on them.…"

"Christian bookstores are a blessing we take for granted in the West," Trevor said. He was an American, responsible for one of the special vehicles used to smuggle Bibles.

Stephen's young friends wanted to know more about my children's books, and I gladly shared my story.

My favorite art in Christian bookstores was Precious Moments, with innocent faces of children. I thought how nice it would be to make Bible storybooks for Romania with this art. I prayed that the Lord would help me.

One day I asked the manager of a bookstore, "Who is this artist? How can I buy his art for Romania?"

He laughed, "You want to buy Samuel Butcher's art! This is big business in the States, and you don't have money." I asked in another bookstore and received the same response.

But I did not give up. In another bookstore I asked an assistant, a helpful girl with a friendly smile. "I can give you the phone number of the company," she said. "I order from their catalogues all the time." She gave me the phone number and, with a prayer in my heart, I dialed the number.

"Hello," I said, "I want to speak to Samuel Butcher."

"You speak with Sam," a man's voice said.

"My name is Genovieva," I said. "I'm so glad you answered the phone. I was exiled from Romania by the communist regime because I taught children about God. I taught them Bible stories and songs. My life was in danger, and I lived in hiding in a church for seven years. The children in Romania don't have anything beautiful to look at. Everything is dull and gray. I would like to do books with beautiful pictures. I like your drawings so much! How much would it cost to buy your art?" I held my breath while I waited for his response.

"I had a sad childhood myself," he said. "My parents separated and I went on the wrong path. One night when I was in a bar, someone came and told me about the love of Jesus, and that His love was for me, too. I gave my life to Him on the spot. Then I put my gift of art on the altar and asked Him to use it. This is when I started to draw this style. I want all the children of the world to know the Lord through my art."

I could hear in Sam's voice that he was very touched. "I will send you a letter to give you permission to use anything I produce for free distribution in Romania," he said. "I also want to help pay for the production of the books."

The young people at the mission house listened intently to my account.

"That's incredible, Genovieva." said Trevor. "Praise the Lord!"

"When did you write the books?" Stephen asked.

"I produced six titles for children in three years: *Căci un Copil ni S-a născut* (For Unto Us a Child is Born), *Hristos a înviat* (Christ is Risen), *Isus e minunat* (Jesus is Wonderful), *Isus mi-a schimbat viața* (Jesus Changed my Life), *În seara de Crăciun și-n alte seri* (On Christmas Eve and Other Evenings) and *Pentru mine* (For Me). As soon as I finished each book, Sam sent me the pictures ready for the printer. He paid thousands of dollars for the color separations. On almost every page was a beautiful picture."

"How did you get the money to pay for the printing?" Diana, the girls' leader, asked as she poured me another cup of coffee.

"In the United States I spoke in many churches and groups about the persecution of Christians in communist Romania. The Lord gave me great favor wherever I went, and people gave enough money for me to have one hundred seventy-five thousand books printed on good quality paper. The Christians who worked at the printer's knew that these books had to be smuggled in because they contained Bible stories and songs that I had composed while hiding in my church in Iaşi. They made a circle around the pallets of books and prayed that they would get safely to the children.

"My brother Teodor was the one who arranged the musical notes for the songs. He also recorded the Sion Children's Choir that I started in Romania. Each book had a cassette with about twenty-five songs from the book."

"I was the one who smuggled the reel-to-reel tapes and the sheets of music out of Romania," Stephen remembered.

"What a blessing that was!" I said. "I then went to a company and had five thousand copies of each cassette made to go with the books. After I printed the books, I met Richard Wurmbrand in a church in Ohio."

"Wasn't he the one who spent fourteen years in prison in Romania for his faith?" asked Becky.

"Yes, that's right," I replied. "He asked me, 'How will you get that many books into Romania? Missions now consider Romania a closed country. The vehicles with special compartments used to smuggle Bibles were caught at the borders.'

"But it was as if his words went in one ear and out the other. I refused to be discouraged. After all, it was the Lord who had helped me produce these books. I heard the Holy Spirit say, '*Is anything too difficult for the Lord, Genovieva?*'"

Stephen nodded and smiled. He and the team knew what it meant to live by faith and to trust the Lord. At that point, the team members surrounded me, laid their hands on me, and prayed for my family in Romania. What a comfort that was!

I prayed that God, who had used me to bring Samuel Butcher's art to the children of Romania, would also use me to rescue my brother from a Romanian prison.

One evening a few days later, Stephen invited me to a restaurant. As we were waiting to be served, I asked him how he got involved in Eastern Europe. The waiter came and took our orders. Soon he brought vegetable soup and Austrian rolls and lit the candle on the table. We thanked the Lord and began to eat, and Stephen told his story while we ate.

Stephen had read *God's Smuggler* by Brother Andrew when he was fifteen. His parents taught him and his three sisters to support missions, giving them collection boxes for different countries. Stephen received a box for Lebanon, but one of his sisters received a box for the Slavic Gospel Association. This mission worked behind the Iron Curtain and helped the persecuted Church, and he suddenly envied her. *Maybe I can exchange my box for hers*, he thought. She agreed and he was very happy.

Five years later, in 1973 when he was a student, Stephen arranged to go on a summer vacation trip to Turkey with Paul and Dave, whom I had also met. He knew they would have to drive through Eastern Europe, so he contacted the local representative of the Slavic Gospel Association in England. He received some addresses in Austria, Yugoslavia, and Romania, and some Serbian Bibles to take to a pastor in Belgrade.

On the way out from England, they stopped in a village near Salzburg in the Austrian Alps. There, at a mission house, they received training on what to expect as they crossed communist borders. The three of them had to be prepared for what would happen to them if they were caught with Bibles: Their vehicle and the literature would be confiscated, and they could be sent to prison. They were taught not to ask for directions, to memorize all their addresses and not to have them written anywhere. They were trained how to make contact with the local believers, as those who received the Bibles from them were in even greater danger.

At the end of the training session, they each answered a questionnaire. The last question was, "What Scripture would you give to the believers in Eastern Europe?" To their surprise they all wrote down the same verses: "Do not be anxious about anything, but in everything, by prayer and petition, with thanksgiving, present your requests to God. And the peace of God, which transcends all understanding, will guard your hearts and your minds in Christ Jesus" (Philippians 4:6–7).

They left Austria in their Volkswagen with the Bibles hidden in the trunk and got through the border into Yugoslavia with no problem. A few days later they arrived in Belgrade and visited Pastor Jakic at his home. They gave him the Serbian Bibles. He and his wife were concerned for the plight of Christians in Romania. They kept a stock of Romanian Bibles in their apartment. While Stephen and his friends were with them, they met John, a young man from England. He also wanted to travel to Romania with Bibles.

Pastor Jakic reminded them of the great need for Bibles in Romania. He asked them if they would be prepared to take a hundred. Stephen talked with Paul and Dave and together they decided they could take forty. John had a bigger car and took a hundred Bibles. The next morning they left Belgrade for the Romanian border. John left some time after them so that they would not arrive at the border at the same time. Stephen assumed he would never meet John again....

In less than an hour Stephen, Paul, and Dave arrived at the border. Stephen drove and they went through Yugoslav passport control and customs with no problem. They crossed into no man's land and stopped at the barrier. After a few minutes it lifted and he drove forward to the Romanian customs point at Moravița. It was almost deserted, except for the soldiers with machine guns. Then a border guard came and took their passports away for inspection. They waited in the car, praying silently.

After about twenty minutes the guard came back.

"Do you have weapons?" he asked Stephen.

"No," he answered.

"Do you have drugs?"

"No."

"Do you have pornography?"

"No."

"Do you have Bibles?"

Stephen nodded, reached behind him for their three English Bibles, and handed them to him. The guard took them away for a long time. Finally, he came back and returned them.

"Open the trunk," he ordered. Stephen's heart beat fast as he got out and opened it. The guard took a quick look inside, then motioned to Stephen that he could close it. He gave them their passports back and waved them through.

Stephen would never forget the joy he felt as the barrier lifted and they entered Romania for the first time. The guards did not find the forty Romanian Bibles hidden under the men's camping equipment.

"That was a miracle," Dave exclaimed as soon as they had crossed the border. The three of them thanked the Lord.

It seemed as if they had gone back fifty years in time. The houses along the sides of the road were painted in bright colors. Ducks and geese, cows and horses, pigs and chickens ran loose in the streets. Storks nested on wagon wheels on the chimney tops. Children smiled and waved at them as they drove by.

The next day they arrived in Râşnov, a small town in the center of the country. They delivered the forty Bibles to a Christian family there.

We finished our meal and the conversation continued. I asked Stephen how he'd gotten my address. He explained that after they had delivered the forty Bibles, they left Romania and crossed into Bulgaria. They went to a campsite for the night. It was late when they arrived and the campsite was full, with hundreds of cars and tents. They drove around a few times and looked for a place to park.

"The only space available is under that lamp," Paul said. "No one wants to park there because of all the insects."

They had no choice but to park their car right there and put up their tent next to it. They tried to sleep, but to no avail. The bugs and beetles crawled into their tent and into their sleeping bags. But little did they know that the Lord had guided them to that very spot.

When they got up the next morning, they saw that they had parked next to another car from England. It was John from Belgrade! They greeted each other in amazement.

"How was your trip to Romania?" Stephen asked him.

"It didn't go well," he said. "They found my Bibles and turned me back into Yugoslavia. But at least they didn't confiscate them. I want to try again from here."

Stephen looked at his passport and saw the word *anulat* stamped in bold letters across his Romanian visa. "You shouldn't try to return to Romania with this passport," he said. "They canceled your visa."

Stephen talked with Paul and Dave, and it was clear to the three of them that this meeting was no coincidence. They believed that the Lord wanted them to go back to Romania with another load of Bibles.

"We could take forty of your Bibles if you give us your contact address," Stephen said.

John found a small piece of paper and wrote on it: "Marcu Nichifor, Strada Sărărie 32, Iaşi." The three of them memorized the address and threw away the piece of paper.

The Lord helped them again to go through the border. After a few days, they arrived in the city of Iaşi. Stephen went into a hotel and found a map of the city. To his surprise, the street they were looking for was clearly marked. He studied how to reach it. They parked the car near the magnificent Palace of Culture in the city center and pretended to be simple tourists. But as soon as it got dark they set off on foot for Strada Sărărie, carrying the forty Bibles in a plastic bag.

They walked up the street and found number thirty-two. It was a church. They pushed open the iron gate, then they tried the front door, but it was locked. They walked around the back. There was no one there.

"Lord," Stephen prayed with Paul and Dave, "please send someone to meet us…to take these Bibles!" As they were wondering what to do, they heard steps…. It was me, Genovieva!

We finished our coffee and I looked at Stephen over the table. We praised the Lord together. I knew that had been a divine appointment.

"Thank you for sharing this story with me," I said. "It strengthens my faith at this difficult time."

How will the Lord rescue my family? I wondered. *Will I ever see them again?*

Chapter Two

The Last Load

The night of Costică's arrest, the children were asleep in their house on Strada Petru Rareş in the center of Iaşi. Teo, six, and Genovieva, four, both looked like their mother. Teo liked to help his father repair cars—perhaps he would one day grow up to become a mechanical engineer like Costică.

My brothers in Iaşi, Romania had been busy that week. They transported thousands of Bibles and children's books to a safe place and now they were tired. Costică and Teodor and their wives, Estera and Erzso, worked night after night and all went well until Friday. They had received and distributed Bibles for many years. But President Nicolae Ceauşescu, with his dreaded Securitate, had declared war against the Bible.

It was the middle of the night and the neighborhood's oak- and fir-lined streets were quiet. Even the dogs were asleep. In the kitchen, behind the curtains, was a little light. There Estera made some strong coffee and served it with a piece of her delicious homemade cake to Costică, Teodor, and Erzso. Estera, a pharmacist, was also a good cook. She knew how to make borscht and *cozonac* for dessert.

In the front yard was a cherry tree in blossom. Costică treasured his beautiful wife, with her warm brown eyes, long, arched brows, and dark hair that hung to her waist. And he admired the way she took good care of their single-story house's flower garden, which had lilies, narcissi, and red and yellow tulips ready to bloom. A low stone wall with an iron fence surrounded the yard. It was a well-loved home, a good home for their family. And Estera loved Costică's curly brown hair, his green eyes, and the smile that was always on his face—as well as his engineer's ability to take care of jobs around the house. In the drive was a Dacia station wagon. It belonged to their pastor, Iosif Morcan, who had lent it to them for that week.

The four of them finished their coffee and went out into the yard. They made a chain from the woodshed to the car. They were tired, and the boxes were heavy.

"Twenty-eight, twenty-nine, thirty boxes," Teodor counted.

"Why don't you stay at home this evening?" Costică suggested to Teodor and Erzso when they were ready to go. "Let me go by myself. Then if anything happens, they will only get me."

"Costică, don't talk like that," said Teodor. "We have worked together for years. We won't let you go on your own. As long as we get back to our flat by three o'clock to get some sleep.… I need to go to work at six."

"Then let's go," Costică whispered as he got in the driver's seat. "I also have to be at work early."

Teodor got in the passenger seat and Erzso in the back.

"Take care and come back soon," Estera said as she opened the gate for them.

"We will be back in a few hours," Costică said. At least that is what he thought.

They drove out quietly and Estera shut the gate behind them.

Teodor and Erzso had been married only a few months. Teodor was short with brown hair and blue eyes. He was a doctor and all his patients loved him because he was kind to them. He would write prescriptions for the poor and pay for them out of his own money. Erzso was an attractive young woman of Hungarian descent, slim with dark eyes and short hair. She studied geography and English at the university. Teodor and Erzso lived in a house a few minutes' walk away on Strada Karl Marx.

"What a blessing these Bibles will be!" Erzso said.

"Yes, what joy we had every time we received a load," Teodor added. "When I first saw the beautiful children's books that Genovieva wrote I cried for joy."

Costică drove slowly along the dark narrow street full of potholes. He rubbed his sleepy eyes.

"Once we get out of the city limit we'll be okay," Teodor said.

As they passed a large house, a dog barked furiously at them. Costică recited a favorite psalm to encourage them. "The LORD is my shepherd, I shall not be in want. He makes me lie down in green pastures, he leads me beside quiet waters, he restores my soul. He guides me in paths of righteousness for his name's sake. Even though I walk through the valley of the shadow of death, I will fear no evil."

Then he turned the corner into Strada Culturii. At that moment a policeman appeared in front of them in the middle of the road. He motioned them to stop.

"Oh, no!" Teodor exclaimed.

"What shall we do?" Erzso panicked.

"You two run away. I will say nothing about you." Costică ordered. "Then go at once and bury the Bibles. I will try to drive away and hide this load in a forest."

Costică pulled in to the side of the road and rolled down the window.

"*Actele la control!* Driver's license and identification," barked the officer. He stared at them as if he knew them.

"What is in those boxes?" he asked. "Open the back for me."

The policeman walked around to the back of the car.

"Let's drive away and escape," Teodor whispered and turned the key in the ignition. The engine turned over but wouldn't start.

They looked at each other, fear on their faces.

Costică tried again and the engine started. The car moved forward a few feet, but then stopped for no reason. It was as if all the powers of darkness were against them that night.

The officer went back to the driver's window.

"So…do you try to escape?" he taunted as he grabbed the key.

Then something strange happened. The officer ran back in the opposite direction as if someone at the end of the road had called his name.

"Run. Run!" Costică urged them.

Teodor and Erzso jumped out of the car, ran to a nearby fence, climbed over it, and escaped into the darkness. They ran across a garden, crossed another fence, and arrived in a back street. All the dogs barked furiously. They walked along back streets and country roads to the hiding place where the Bibles were stored.

The officer returned to the car with a taxi driver as a witness. Costică was taken into custody at the secret police headquarters where the Sfatcu family had been interrogated many times for possessing the Bible, the Word of God.

———————————

It was lunchtime again that spring day at the mission house in Vienna. The cook brought sausages and rice for the team of Bible smugglers. It smelled delicious, but I could hardly eat. I straightened my hair, tied up with a velvet hair band that matched my blue dress. I thought of my family in their distress. Stephen sat across from me at the table. He wore his wool sweater and corduroy trousers. I looked at him, and his peaceful eyes comforted me.

"I feel that President Ceaușescu took revenge on me," I said. "I spoke in almost every state in America about the plight of Christians in Romania. In 1980 after I gave a newspaper interview in New York, a Romanian spy called me and threatened me on the phone. 'Don't speak about persecution in Romania,' he said. 'If you do we will cut your throat, put you in a garbage bag, and throw you in a Dumpster. No one will ever know what happened to you.'"

"That sounds scary," Trevor exclaimed.

"Another time I spoke in Indiana," I continued. "In the meeting there was an old man who listened to me with great interest. He was a tall, heavy man with thick glasses. After the meeting he took me aside and said, 'I saw your picture and the ad in the newspaper. You are a good speaker. I am retired from the CIA and I know all about the evil of communism. Your name is on the communists' hit list. I would advise you to move every three months.'

"'Thank you very much,' I said. 'But the Lord tells me in the Bible "to speak up for those who cannot speak for themselves" (Proverbs 31:8). He protected me in Romania and He will protect me here too.'"

By this time the young people at the mission had finished their lunch.

Becky brought apples for everyone. She turned to me and said, "Now I understand why you feel responsible for what happened to your family. You risked your life to help others. The Lord said, 'Whoever wants to save his life will lose it, but whoever loses his life for me and for the gospel will save it' (Mark 8:35). So though it seems without hope right now the Lord will fulfill His Word."

"Thank you," I said. "I needed that."

I went on to tell a story that happened in the spring of 1984. I had been invited to speak in a Mennonite church in Ohio. The people were dressed plain. An Amish girl, Rachel, accompanied me in the car to the evening meeting. About 150 people came to the old church building and sat down on the wooden benches. They sang a few songs then the pastor called me up to the front. I spoke about the persecution of believers as usual. Everyone listened to me attentively. As I spoke, I noticed a strange couple on the last bench. He was a big man and looked Romanian, but was dressed in a black high-collar Mennonite suit. She was small and stocky with a plain dress and a cape and had short hair under a white Amish bonnet. As I spoke, I felt that they were not with me. During my testimony, he got up and went outside for a while.

What is he up to? I wondered.

The service lasted about two hours, and afterward I drove home with Rachel on a lonely country road. But after a couple of miles my new car suddenly stopped. I got out and raised the hood.

Just then a car stopped alongside us. To my horror it was the strange couple. The man opened the window, looked at me, and asked, "Do you need help?"

"Yes," I said.

He got out and took a few minutes to check the engine.

"I can't help you now," he said. "You will have to take it to a garage. Come in our car and we will take you home."

"No, thank you," I said.

"Please come with us," his wife insisted.

"No, I really can't."

Then the man looked me in the eye and said in perfect Romanian, "I know who you are."

"And I know who you are too," I said. "You are a Romanian spy and you work for the Romanian Embassy."

I felt trapped. Rachel took my hand in fear, and I prayed in a low voice, "Lord, help us!"

At that moment I saw headlights approaching. A car stopped and pulled up next to us. It was a young couple from the meeting. The Romanians then got into their car and drove off.

"That's Genovieva," I heard.

"Can we help you?" the wife asked.

I explained to them what had happened. He looked under the hood of my car, found a loose wire, and reconnected it.

"Someone must have done that on purpose," he said.

After that my car was fine. We arrived home about midnight.

The young people listened with great interest.

"So Ceauşescu had his Securitate everywhere," said Stephen.

"And the Lord has His angels everywhere too," said Diana.

On another occasion, in September 1984, I was on a speaking trip in the Florida panhandle. I stayed with an old couple. I noticed that a man watched me from his car outside the house where I stayed.

The church that invited me advertised my schedule in newspapers and on television. On the Sunday afternoon, Lynn, a girl in her twenties, came to take me to the meeting that evening. Three other girls came with us in the car. I sat in the front seat with Lynn and we left at five o'clock. I saw that the car in front of the house followed us.

We set off on a straight two-lane road with forests on both sides. The girls talked about their schools and boyfriends, but I was in my own world. *What is the man up to?* I wondered.

I kept an eye on the mirror and prayed in my heart. As I prayed, I sensed that a presence came in the car. Peace flooded my heart, and I knew an angel came to protect me.

There were no other vehicles in sight, apart from the car behind us. Then I saw a pickup truck coming from the opposite direction. As it got closer, I saw that it had enormous wheels and that there were at least two men in it. The man in the car behind talked on a walkie-talkie with the men in the truck and then overtook us. At that point, the truck steered into our lane and accelerated straight into our path.

"What is he doing?" Lynn screamed.

The girls cried out in terror. Lynn drove onto the shoulder, then into the ditch. The truck missed us, but turned and came after us in the ditch and tried to hit us from behind. We almost overturned, but Lynn skillfully maneuvered the car back onto the road.

By this time other vehicles appeared on the road, and the truck sped away in the opposite direction.

"I've never been so scared in all my life," Lynn said.

"We could all have been killed," said another girl.

I knew the Lord had saved me again. Lynn dropped me off at the church. She then went with the other girls to the police to report the incident. The FBI told me later that they knew there was a communist cell in the area and that some of the members had tried to kill me.

The Americans on the team were fascinated by this story.

"How far the communists will go to silence those who expose them!" Becky said.

"I continued to speak in churches because it was the only way I could help my people with Bibles and food. Now it is my family who are in trouble, and I feel responsible for them."

"Genovieva, I understand how you feel," Stephen said. "I also feel responsible for what happened because I helped to arrange the delivery of the Bibles."

"Thank you, Stephen," I said. "That makes my burden lighter."

After we first met in 1973, Stephen continued to travel to Eastern Europe almost every year with Bibles. In 1981 he joined the mission in Austria. That is when he started to take large quantities of Bibles, thousands at a time. Altogether, he went to Romania eighteen times during Ceauşescu's dictatorship. My family was among his best contacts, and I knew he had been to see them recently.

He visited Teodor on that trip, traveling with another young man from England, Roger. At that time there was a nationwide ban on the use of private vehicles in order to conserve energy. Only official and foreign vehicles were allowed.

I asked Stephen how my family was. I hadn't seen them for five years because, as he knew, I could not go back to Romania.

They were all doing well. They told him that Bibles were scarce in the country and that children's books were almost nonexistent. He met with them at Costică and Estera's house. Teodor, Erzso, and my mother came to see him there too. They all asked about me. They also had a lot of business to talk about. Stephen asked Costică and Teodor if they could handle a large load of a few thousand Bibles. Teodor assured him they could, and asked if he could take out some films and cassettes for me. He agreed, as they had a good hiding place in the van. Teodor said he would have another cassette of the children's choir if he could return after a couple of days.

They left my family and returned to their van, which was parked by the Palace of Culture in the center of the city. They had only driven a short distance when they had to stop for a flat tire. It was too late to have it repaired that night, so they had no choice but to spend the night in the van by the side of the road.

In the morning a repair truck "happened" to stop and offer to help. The man repaired the tire, but Stephen noticed he looked guilty, as if he knew who had caused the damage.

That evening they arrived in Piatra-Neamţ and visited Victor Tărniceriu, my friend Silvia's brother. They parked the van in the shadows round the back of the block and walked up a flight of stairs to the apartment. Victor and his wife, Mihaela, welcomed them warmly. Mihaela served each of them a cup of mint tea and a piece of cheese pie. Then they talked business with Victor. He gladly agreed to take a large load of Bibles. Just then there was a knock at the door. Victor looked to see who it was.

"Quick," he whispered. "Hide in the bedroom and keep quiet. It's the secret police."

They stood still behind the closed door and listened. *Is this the end? Will they arrest us? What will happen to Victor?* Stephen wondered.

Once the secret police had left, they came out and Victor explained. "They asked for the so-called guest book," he said. "You are supposed to write the names and addresses of any visitors, relatives included, even if they stay for only ten minutes. If you do not fill it up and they catch you, you can be fined three months' salary."

Stephen understood that the Securitate was after them. He knew they had to get out of there fast. Victor told them when it was safe to leave, and they quickly ran down the stairs and out of the block to their van. They did not see anyone around, but as they started up and headed out on the road back to Iaşi, a car followed them. It often kept less than a hundred yards behind them. They stopped at a hotel for the night in the town of Roman. When they set out the next morning, the car was behind them again. Stephen decided they should not try to go back to Teodor, but head for the Hungarian border, two days' drive away.

It was easy to see that they were being followed, because there were practically no other vehicles on the roads. He noticed that the Securitate used a different car in each county they traveled through. When they arrived in Cluj, they stopped outside a *cofetărie* to buy some cakes. The four men in the red Dacia that followed them stopped on the other side of the road. They seemed frantic in case they lost them. Roger went over to their car, offered them a cake and said, "We have driven together for so long, we might as well share dessert!" But they pretended they did not understand.

When they arrived at the border, one of the guards asked Stephen, "Did you have any problems?"

"Oh, just a flat tire," he said with a smile.

Then the officer came up to their vehicle and ordered, "Everything out!"

They took out all their personal belongings from the vehicle, including the hidden films and cassettes. The guards then did a thorough search of the van. They checked their belongings and wallets as well.

"Drive up the ramp for a vehicle inspection," one of them ordered.

They spent a good half an hour examining the structure of the vehicle. They were very frustrated when they found nothing.

They crossed the border safely and returned to their base in Vienna. Again and again, the Lord saved Stephen at the borders.

"Stephen, what you brought out on that trip was very important for me and for the work," I said.

"Take courage, Genovieva," he said. "The Lord will save your family.…"

My thoughts were back with my trouble. *Where are Costică, Teodor and the rest of my family? What can I do to rescue them?*

Costică,
Estera,
Teo, and
Genovieva,
1982

The prison in
Iaşi where
Costică was held
from July to
September 1985

Teodor and Erzso
Sfatcu, summer
1985

Chapter Three

A Night of Interrogation

The night of April 19, 1985, Costică arrived at Iaşi's secret police headquarters in the backseat of a police car. He got out, his hands handcuffed behind his back. Another police officer brought the pastor's car and unloaded the boxes onto a table in the yard. He counted the Bibles and children's books in front of Costică. Then he wrote the report: "Constantin Sfatcu was caught transporting 600 Bibles, 200 children's books and 500 Scripture cards by car." Costică signed the declaration and the taxi driver also signed as a witness.

From there Costică was led through the back entrance, down a corridor to the interrogation room. Two officers waited for him there. It was a large room with a parquet floor and a window opposite the door. On the right a man in plain clothes sat at a desk, on which were a telephone and some files. Next to it was an armchair and a metal filing cabinet. On the wall was a large portrait of President Ceauşescu. In the far left corner on a pole hung a blue, gold, and red Romanian flag. Costică sat down on a hard wooden bench in front of the desk, still dressed in his green corduroy suit.

"You had bad luck tonight, didn't you?" Aldea, the plainclothes officer said.

"President Ceauşescu personally ordered us to arrest you," said Negru. He was in his mid-thirties and he wore a khaki suit and tie. "Don't you know that the president started his war against the Bible right here in Iaşi…and to be caught with Bibles is a great crime."

"At the top of the wanted list was your brother, Teodor. You were number two. And finally you are both in our hands," Aldea said, rubbing his hands together with glee.

Did they arrest Teodor too? Costică wondered.

"Where did you get the Bibles?" Negru asked as he straightened his glasses.

"Some foreigners brought them," Costică replied, his face pale.

Costică thought about his wife and children. *What will Estera tell them in the morning when they wake up?* He remembered how he'd kissed them good night the evening before.

Negru walked back and forth, his back straight, his hands in his pockets, showing off his communist decorations.

"What are the names of the foreigners?" he asked.

"Er…Micky, Nicky, and Ricky," Costică answered.

"Are you mocking us?" Aldea asked.

"They didn't tell me their full names."

"You brother is in the next room," Negru said. "Tell us the truth."

"He will be asked the same questions. If your answers do not match, you will be finished," Aldea shouted.

The thought that his brother was also under arrest was hard to bear. *Lord, help us!* Costică prayed.

"Where did the foreigners come from?" Aldea continued.

"I think they had an Austrian van," Costică replied.

"What was the registration number?"

"I don't know."

"What nationality were they?" Negru asked.

"I spoke English with them."

"What organization did they work with?" Aldea asked.

"They never told me."

There was a knock at the door, and an officer on duty brought a silver tray with two bottles of cold Pepsi, two cups of coffee, and two pieces of chocolate cake. The interrogators served themselves. Costică received only a glass of tap water.

He remembered when he was a student of mechanical engineering at the University of Iaşi. One evening his family received a load of Bibles from Open Doors, Brother Andrew's mission in Holland. Two girls, Atti and Patti, came with a van. They drove up to the house in the dark and unloaded thick, black plastic sacks full of Bibles. They prayed briefly with the family and left. An hour later they came back; Atti said they had a mechanical problem and asked him to help. He went with them to a forest where their van was parked in a lay-by on a quiet road. They were supposed to activate a mechanism that opened secret compartments in the walls. The system had gone wrong, and they couldn't close them properly. Costică managed to repair the mechanism, and the girls went on their way safely. That was the first time he had seen a Bible-smuggling van.

As far as the last load of Bibles was concerned, everything was very secretive. He did not know where they came from or how they got into the country. And he was glad he didn't.

"So, what were the names of the foreigners?" Aldea asked after he finished his coffee.

"I told you I don't know."

"How old were they?" asked Negru.

"They were all about my age."

"How did the Bibles get into the country?" continued Aldea.

"I don't know."

"You have to confess because we know more than you think," Aldea threatened. "I will prove it to you: One evening you were in the pastor's yard. You said you would drive from there to the hiding place where the Bibles were stored. Then you said you would leave the Bibles there until they could be distributed.…"

How did they know? Costică wondered.

"Listen to this tape," Aldea said and started a cassette player.

Then they played a tape of conversations he'd had with Teodor and with the foreigners who brought the Bibles. Despite the fact that sensitive matters were always talked about in whispers, they were clearly recorded.

"What made you think you could get away with it?" Aldea shouted.

All night long Costică was interrogated. His wrists hurt from the handcuffs. *There is no hope for me,* he thought.

When morning came he was taken to a cell in the basement of the secret police headquarters. He strengthened himself in the Lord with

Psalm 23: "You are with me; your rod and your staff, they comfort me. You prepare a table before me in the presence of my enemies. You anoint my head with oil; my cup overflows. Surely goodness and love will follow me all the days of my life, and I will dwell in the house of the LORD for ever." Then he fell asleep on the hard bed.

While her husband was being interrogated, Estera was in bed, but she could not sleep. She got up and went to the children's bedroom. They were asleep, hugging their toys in their beds. She left their bedroom door half open and stepped quietly into the living room. She knelt down by the window, her favorite place, and looked out at the beautiful starry sky.

Where is Costică? she wondered.

When midnight came and Costică did not return, Estera suddenly sensed that something was wrong. *Was he arrested, beaten or even killed?* She started to cry, unable to stop.

"Lord, take this fear away," she prayed. "I am so afraid that I will never see him again."

The grandfather clock struck one. She got up from the window and went into the kitchen. She made herself a cup of hot milk with honey. *This will be good to calm me down,* she thought. She walked back and forth, wiping her tears away. She tried to sleep on the couch, but in vain. She called Teodor and Erzso's number and let the phone ring and ring…but there was no reply. When dawn came she tried again, but still no reply.

At eight o'clock she called the police station.

"My husband is missing. His name is Constantin Sfatcu."

The officer on duty checked the nightly reports. He came back a few minutes later and said, "He is not here."

"Can you check with the chief?" Estera insisted.

"I suggest you inquire at the hospital first," he answered.

Estera called Emergency.

"Constantin Sfatcu? Let me check," the clerk said. "No…no one by that name was admitted last night. If you checked with the police already, inquire at the morgue."

She called the morgue. Her heart beat fast. *Is he dead or alive?* After a few minutes a voice said, "No, he is not here."

Estera's mother, Ileana, stayed with the children while Estera took her purse and went to the police station. It was a twenty-minute walk. The police and the Securitate had their offices in a three-story building. She explained to the officer on duty at the main entrance that she still could not find her husband. She asked to speak to the chief of police, and he escorted her to his office.

Estera knocked at the door and entered an elegantly furnished room. The chief of police, Zaharia, was at his office desk in a plush armchair. For a few moments he ignored her, then he turned to her.

"Where is my husband?" she asked.

"He is in our hands," he admitted. "We arrested him last night. He tried to murder a policeman," he said with an air of satisfaction.

"That can't be true!" Estera exclaimed.

There was a knock at the door, and Bădărău, the chief prosecutor, came in. "You are Mrs. Sfatcu, aren't you?" he said.

Estera nodded.

"Your husband has already confessed to the crime," Bădărău continued. "He has signed a declaration of guilt. He will get between fifteen and twenty years."

"That is not true. That is not true!" Estera gasped. "Your accusations are false."

Estera burst into tears, but they just laughed at her. She left the office and ran home weeping uncontrollably, not caring that people stared at her.

When she arrived home, she explained to her mother what happened.

"What shall I say to the children?" Estera asked her.

"The Lord will give you the right words," Ileana replied. "I will get the breakfast ready."

Ileana laid the table, put oatmeal in bowls, and poured boiled milk over it for the children. She made scrambled eggs with tomatoes for all of them.

"Where is Dad?" asked Teo as he came into the kitchen in his pajamas. He sat on his chair at the table, and his sister sat next to him.

"Some bad policemen arrested your dad," Estera answered. "He did not do anything wrong. Do you remember the story of Joseph that I read to you from the Bible?"

Teo and Genovieva nodded, their mouths full of food.

"Joseph was arrested and put in prison for something he did not do. The same thing happened to your father. We should pray that Jesus brings him back to us soon."

"Can we go and see him?" asked four-year-old Genovieva.

"Not right now," Estera said, her heart pierced with grief.

Estera knelt down, and her mother and the children followed her in a prayer, "Lord, bless our dad. Take care of him. Let him have food and clothes. Don't let the bad people hurt him, and bring him home quickly! Amen."

News of Costică's arrest traveled fast, and soon friends filled the home. Day and night brothers and sisters in the Lord came to comfort her. They read Scriptures to her and prayed with her. One day Lenuța Roman, an intercessor in the church, read a Scripture to her. "I consider that our present sufferings are not worth comparing with the glory that will be revealed in us.… Who shall separate us from the love of Christ? Shall trouble or hardship or persecution or famine or nakedness or danger or sword?… No, in all these things we are more than conquerors through him who loved us" (Romans 8:18, 35, 37).

Friends from the church came and brought food and flowers for Estera. The next day was Sunday, and she went to church with the children. Pastor Iosif Morcan prayed for Costică from the pulpit, that he would be strong and all the Sfatcu family would be comforted.

Every prayer, every song, every Scripture meant so much to her. Some committed themselves to fast for Costică two days a week. The church decided to have prayer meetings for the Sfatcu family every evening.

Estera received telephone calls and telegrams from inside and outside the country. Everyone assured her that she was not alone in this trial.

At this time, I was still in Vienna. As long as I was with other believers to encourage me I was all right, but when I went to bed I cried a lot. I imagined Costică and Teodor in chains, hungry and cold and beaten by the Securitate.

I received the news that my friends in Switzerland had organized a campaign of writing cards of comfort to my family. They also sent cards of protest to the Romanian Embassy in Bern. That encouraged me. I knew the communists did everything in the dark and when they were exposed, they would run. I wanted the whole world to know about my family.

From Austria I returned home to the United States. I called my friend, Char Binkley, who was the director of a Christian radio station. She had interviewed me on the radio several times about my life in Romania. *Lord, use Char to spread the word around*, I prayed. And the Lord heard my prayer....

Char interviewed me regarding my family. Some supporters ordered the cassette of the interview from the radio station. It got into the hands of Congressman Tom Riner. He and his wife sent me word that they were with me in my trouble. They made a copy of the cassette and sent it to Senator Gene Huff in Kentucky. He was also a Pentecostal pastor who represented the suffering church in Washington, DC.

Senator Huff and his wife invited me to stay with them in Kentucky for a week. They gave me a lovely room in their home. Ethel even made Romanian stuffed cabbage and baked fresh rolls especially for me. They comforted and encouraged me and prayed with me for my family. I also spoke in their church and shared my burden.

Senator Huff was on the board of Christian Solidarity International. This organization put a full-page article in the *New York Times* on May 13, 1985, showing pictures of my brothers Costică and Teodor. It was an open letter to President Ceaușescu, protesting their arrest and calling for their immediate release.

Of course, the *New York Times* went all over the world, and Christians everywhere prayed for my family.

Oh, how good is the Lord!

AN OPEN LETTER TO
PRESIDENT NICOLAE CEAUSESCU,
BUCHAREST, ROMANIA

Dear President Ceausescu,

We are deeply concerned with the recent imprisonment and mistreatment of Constantin Sfatcu, of Iasi, Romania, who was arrested by police for possession of Christian literature. We fear, as in past cases, false charges will be fabricated against him. Teodor Sfatcu is also being implicated in this case. This is clearly in violation of the Helsinki Final Act, which recognizes the "freedom of the individual to profess and practise, alone or in community with others, religion or belief acting in accordance with the dictates of his own conscience."

The American people cherish this freedom to worship as they choose, as an inherent right of every individual. This freedom is jealously guarded by the American people. They cannot rest while others are being denied this basic human right.

Mr. President, we hope the case of Constantin and Teodor Sfatcu will be resolved quickly. This action, we feel, would be looked upon favorably by the United States Congress as it begins its annual discussion of Most-Favored-Nation trade status for Romania.

Sincerely,
CHRISTIAN RESPONSE INTERNATIONAL

DEAR AMERICAN CITIZEN,
YOUR CONCERN CAN MAKE A DIFFERENCE!
YOU CAN HELP CONSTANTIN AND TEODOR SFATCU BY:

1. CALLING AND WRITING PRESIDENT REAGAN, asking him to consider the 1985 renewal of Most-Favored-Nation trade status for Romania. (An agreement giving Romania significant trade benefits with the U.S., thus bolstering the Romanian economy). Please call and write:

PRESIDENT RONALD REAGAN
THE WHITE HOUSE
1600 Pennsylvania Avenue N.W.
Washington, D.C. 20500
(202) 456-7639

2. EXPRESSING YOUR CONCERN TO YOUR CONGRESSMEN about the case of Constantin and Teodor Sfatcu. Ask them to consider the gross violation of human rights at the upcoming Most-Favored-Nation trade status hearings. All U.S. Senators and Representatives can be called at (202) 224-3121.

3. CALLING AND WRITING THE ROMANIAN EMBASSY IN WASHINGTON, D.C., asking for the immediate release of Constantin Sfatcu and an end to the harassment of Teodor Sfatcu. Please call and write to the following:

Ambassador Nicolae Gavrilescu
Embassy of the S.R. of Romania
1607 23rd Street N.W.
Washington, D.C. 20008
(202) 232-4747
(202) 232-4722

 CHRISTIAN RESPONSE INTERNATIONAL
Box 24042 • Washington, D.C. 20024 • Phone (801) 984-9707

Open letter to President Ceaușescu in support of Constantin and
Teodor Sfatcu, placed in the *New York Times,* May 13, 1985

Chapter Four

Burying Bibles

After they escaped from the car the night of the arrest, Teodor and Erzso reached the hiding place where the Bibles were stored. They dug a hole, put the Bibles in plastic bags, and buried them in the ground. Then they covered the earth with a pile of firewood. It took them all that night. When they finished, they walked back to their apartment in Iaşi, where their car was parked. They got in and drove to Mama's house on Strada George Coşbuc.

It was still early, but Mama, a stocky woman in her mid-sixties, was up and dressed in her house coat in the kitchen.

"What happened?" she asked as they entered the house.

"The police stopped us last night," Teodor whispered. "Costică was caught with Bibles and arrested."

"Oh, no!" Her dark eyes filled with alarm.

"He told us to run away," said Erzso. "We escaped and went to hide the rest of the Bibles."

"Mama, tell the others to hide their Bibles too, and send a message to uncle Avram," Teodor continued.

"Yes, yes, of course," she said. "I will let them know."

Mama lived with two of her grandchildren, Corina and Iulian, whom she had raised since they were small. They were still asleep in the bedroom.

She had just done her spring cleaning, and her house was spotless. The big wooden clock on the kitchen wall ticked solemnly, and a vase of red and yellow tulips from her garden stood on the table, their bright colors seeming bold and courageous in this frightening time. The old wool carpet with blue and pink roses woven into the pattern was worn but clean.

"Quick, have something to eat," said Mama. "I baked plenty of sweet bread with walnuts and vanilla. You never know when you will eat again." She shook her close-cropped gray head and gave them each a cup of coffee with boiled milk. "You both look so tired."

Teodor and Erzso ate and drank in a hurry.

"Get out of town quickly and hide," she told them. "Soon they will come to arrest you too." Mama hugged them. "May the Lord protect you," she said as they got into the car.

Teodor and Erzso tried to drive out of town as quickly as possible.

"Let's go on Strada Păcurar and get to Târgu Frumos," Teodor suggested. They drove down the hill…but after five minutes they saw police ahead.

"Let's try the road to Vaslui," Erzso said as Teodor turned the car around. They drove the mile back up the hill to the main road, but police blocked that route too.

Teodor tried a third road that could get them out of town, but the police were everywhere.

"Let's drive through the forest," he said. "It's our last chance."

They drove along a muddy, narrow track, full of potholes, around bushes and trees, only to find that it led nowhere. They turned back and returned to Mama's house.

Soon the house searches started. Six men went to Estera's house and searched it room by room. They confiscated all Bibles and Christian literature. Another six men arrived at Mama's house and did the same there.

Suddenly, another secret police car with six more men arrived at Mama's house, and an officer got out and knocked at the door. Teodor opened the door.

"*Buletinele la control!*" the officer demanded. He checked Teodor's and Erzso's identification. "You two are under arrest. We have a search warrant. Take us to your apartment."

Teodor and Erzso drove to their apartment on Strada Karl Marx, and the secret police car followed them. It was a two-room apartment on the first floor in a semidetached house. Teodor opened the door and let in their unwanted guests.

There was a mirror in the hall, under which Teodor and Erzso left their shoes. The living room was spacious, and cotton carpets covered the floors. Pictures of their wedding adorned the walls, alongside original paintings by Maria Lazăr, an artist in the church. Teodor's piano stood across the room from their couch and two armchairs. His cello occupied a corner by itself. Along one wall a bookcase held hundreds of books. The kitchen was small, but the pantry was full of pickles and jars of strawberry and cherry jam made by Erzso.

Among the six men were the chief of police in Iaşi, the chief prosecutor, a colonel in the secret police, another officer, and two witnesses.

The chief prosecutor told them, "Make a declaration of all foreign and Romanian currency in your possession."

To possess foreign currency or large amounts of Romanian money was a criminal offence and would have resulted in serious charges against them.

"I have no foreign currency and only two months' salary," Teodor answered.

Thank God that I gave out all the money to those in need a few days ago. Lord, protect us! Don't let them find that list and those notes.

The officers started their search with the bookcase. They each took one book at a time, paging through it and looking for notes and papers. They searched through diaries, notebooks, and photo albums. They also read all Teodor's and Erzso's letters, one by one.

They continually made and received calls, and received and gave orders. It was clear that they communicated with the secret police in Bucharest. The Sfatcu family's case was regarded as a serious one, and their plight would be decided by the highest authorities.

The officers now checked a shelf where Teodor and Erzso had hidden the list of names. The chief of police snatched it and held it up.

"Look at this," the chief of police said to the prosecutor.

Oh Lord! Teodor thought. *Why did You allow them to find those papers?*

They were notes written by his hand, a record of how he used money entrusted to him by me. It was a list of names of believers from all over Romania who received money, the amounts received, and their signatures. They also found some confidential notes from churches, signed by elders, acknowledging gifts. The secret police looked at these papers with satisfaction and considered them a valuable acquisition. They carefully put them aside on the table with other confiscated material.

Teodor looked at those notes on the table. The Lord did not answer his prayer. At least that is what he thought.… He knew there was enough evidence there to send him to prison. It was forbidden to help persecuted believers. That list with signatures was also proof that a lot of cash went through his hands.

"Let's have a break," the colonel said after a few hours. He turned to Erzso and asked, "Can we go out onto your balcony to smoke?"

"Yes, of course," she replied. "Would you like a piece of cheesecake and a glass of apple juice?"

"Thank you," the colonel said.

Three of the officers went out on the balcony to smoke. A few minutes later Erzso took a tray of refreshments out to them. She set it on the picnic table where the men sat and with a smile she said, "Help yourselves!"

The officer who remained with the witnesses inside the apartment concentrated on reading through other papers. They seemed tired. Erzso also brought them cheesecake and juice. At that moment Teodor caught Erzso's eye and understood.

"Thank you," the officer said with obvious delight, his mouth full of cheesecake.

Then, in a second, Teodor grabbed the list and the notes from the table and ran with them to the bathroom. He tore the papers into pieces, threw them into the toilet, then flushed it. The next moment he was out again and back in the room.

One of the witnesses noticed and whispered something to the officer. The officer thought that Teodor hid something on his body and on the spot gave him a thorough search. He looked in every pocket, in the lining of his clothes, even in his shoes and socks—but of course, he found nothing.

Another fifteen minutes went by, and the three men came back in from the balcony. The search went on in the same detailed manner for another four hours. At half past ten that night, when they finished, they drove Teodor and Erzso to the police station. Teodor and Erzso did not think they would be free again. However, by midnight, after signing declarations concerning the material confiscated, they were allowed to go home. The next day was Sunday, and they went to church. The building was packed. All the church knew what had happened. The brothers and sisters prayed for a long time, with many tears, for Costică, Estera, Teodor, Erzso, Mama, and for the whole Sfatcu family. They comforted them with words from the Bible and carried the burden of their suffering. But there was a heavy presence of secret police in the pews. They had angry faces, and didn't like the encouragement given to the Sfatcu family. What were they up to?

<hr />

In June 1985 I stayed with a friend of mine, Veronica Şuşman, who lived near Akron, Ohio. She lived in a small white house with a porch full of red geraniums, which were as colorful as her nicely ironed clothes and as neat as her braided white hair under her scarf. Though in her seventies, she was still a tall, well-built woman who took great care of her vegetable garden, where she grew rows of lettuces, green onions, parsley, dill, cucumbers and tomatoes. The garden had cherry trees with a big crop of ripe cherries. There was a wooden bench in her garden and I sat down there to read my Bible and pray for my family. It was so beautiful there, but my heart was so sad. I cried so much for my family in Romania.

"Lunch is ready, Genovieva," Veronica called.

"I am coming," I said. I went into the house and sat down on an old wooden chair at the kitchen table.

"I have prepared pea stew with dill and salad from the garden," she said.

I had hardly any appetite. "I will only have a small bowl today, thank you."

My thoughts were with my family in Romania. *Do they have any food, even a piece of bread? Do they have any water?*

"Genovieva," Veronica told me one evening, "I have never seen anyone cry so much. You need to trust the Lord."

Soon after the open letter to Ceaușescu was published in the May 13 issue of the *New York Times* on behalf of my family, I noticed a car outside Veronica's house. I recognized a Romanian spy in it. The car followed me wherever I went.

"Don't go out by yourself," Veronica said. "I will come with you everywhere."

One evening in my bedroom, with tears in my eyes, I knelt down and looked up through the window at the stars in the sky. I asked the Lord to speak to me. Then I opened the Bible and read: "Some faced jeers and flogging, while still others were chained and put in prison. They were stoned; they were sawed in two; they were put to death by the sword. They went about in sheepskins and goatskins, destitute, persecuted and mistreated—the world was not worthy of them" (Hebrews 11:36–38). I read this Scripture and tried to accept whatever would happen to my family.

———————

Estera and the children were encouraged by the love of many, expressed in visits, gifts, phone calls, and letters. But soon the secret police made sure all that brought her comfort was cut off from her.

The secret police called her friends one by one and warned them not to visit her anymore—or they would get into trouble. Gradually the number of those who dared to visit her became quite small. The telephone line to her house was cut, as were the telephone lines of about thirty of her relatives and friends. No one could encourage her through phone calls anymore. The secret police also stopped her mail, and a sense of isolation descended upon her. But no one could cut off the prayers, and the prayers sustained her.

One morning Estera was called to the courthouse to bring a parcel of clothes for her husband. She put on her new cotton dress. Because she had fasted, the dress was too big for her. She looked in the mirror and combed her long, dark hair. Mama went with her. She too wore her best dress and high-heeled shoes. Mama was usually cheerful, but now she could not even smile. They walked the half mile to the courthouse.

"We came to bring this parcel of clothes for my husband, Constantin Sfatcu," Estera told the officer on duty when they arrived.

"Constantin Sfatcu?" the officer repeated. "See those chairs at the end of the hall? Wait there and someone will come and take your parcel."

They walked to the end of the long corridor and sat down on the chairs. Nearby, a door bore a sign: Criminal Section. They waited there for fifteen minutes.

"Do you think we will see Costică?" Mama asked.

"I don't think so," Estera replied.

Little did they know....

Suddenly the door opened and a man in handcuffs come out, his face swollen and bruised. An officer escorted him. At first they did not recognize him. Then he met Estera's eyes.

"Costică! Costică!" Estera screamed. She jumped up and stretched her arms toward him.

"My son! My son!" Mama shouted. She held her head in her hands and burst into tears.

"You are not allowed to talk to him," the officer said. "Leave the parcel here and go home!" Immediately a policeman escorted them from the building.

They walked home arm in arm, wiping away their tears.

"They planned it very well so as to add to our grief," Estera said.

"Yes, to see him treated like a criminal. His only crime was to distribute the Word of God," replied Mama, sobbing.

One evening while I was in Veronica's home, we sat in soft armchairs and I shared with her the story of the night a van full of Bibles got stuck before it even left the church gates.

It happened in the winter of 1978 in Iaşi, Romania. The Bible was a forbidden book and the only way to obtain one was through courageous Bible smugglers from the West. I was twenty-seven at the time and I lived at the church in semi-hiding.

I had been a contact for Bible smugglers for years. God had protected me. I had the courage to die for the Lord. At least I thought I had, until that December night.

The secret police had warned me several times during interrogations, "If we catch you with Bibles—even just a few—we will put you in chains."

"Catch me," I would reply calmly. The smartly dressed officer couldn't help noticing the peaceful look on my face.

It was now midnight. Strada Sărărie was quiet. Even the dogs were asleep. The windows of all the houses were dark, and snow fell softly. Fir trees shrouded the gray church building. It seemed as quiet as the other houses from the front. The heavy curtains were drawn and the gates were locked. But at the back of the church we worked hard in the dark, as quietly as we could.

"How many have you got?" I asked Charlie, the stocky, bald Danish brother, as he handed me heavy black garbage bags full of Bibles and New Testaments.

"About four thousand," he replied. "Can you take them all?" He spoke broken English.

"Yes," I said in a whisper. "There is such a great need!"

I was always amazed at the number of Bibles they could hide in a camper van. I knew "Charlie" was not his real name. His wife, "Mary," handed the bags out from the back of the van. My brother, Teodor, and our friend, Elena, put them in the woodshed. The Bible smugglers never gave their real names or addresses. It was better for everyone, in case we were caught. They would unload the Bibles as quickly as possible then head for the border.

"Couriers like to come to you, Genovieva," Charlie said, "because you are always ready to take the whole load. It makes it so much easier for us not to need to go to different places. Here, these blue thick bags contain Russian Bibles. Do you want them?"

"Oh, yes! You can leave them here. I have a way to get them over the border. It is just a few miles from here."

"You are so courageous," Charlie said.

"Give our love and prayers to all those who send us Bibles," I said. "We pray for you all every day. Everyone wants Bibles in Romania. A doctor would even accept one in payment for a surgery."

"Forty-five…fifty bags. We are almost done," Charlie whispered from inside the camper.

Mary handed us some apples and nuts, and we received them gratefully.

"Now we will push the van out without starting the engine so as not to wake up the neighbors," I said. "In a few minutes you will be out of here."

But little did I know what lay ahead of us.

As we pushed the camper round the corner toward the front of the church, it got stuck. The front wheels were jammed between the concrete drive and a thick tree stump. Fear gripped me.

Then I remembered a friend from another town, brother Dumitru, whose car had gotten stuck in the mud while full of Bibles. He was overwhelmed with fear and started to tremble. An angel appeared to him and said, "Do not be afraid! Many angels are protecting this work."

Oh Lord, I prayed, *please send us an angel too!*

We joined hands in prayer, asking the Lord to intervene. "It is written, 'The angel of the LORD encamps around those who fear him, and he delivers them,'" (Psalm 34:7) I prayed. But the van remained immobile.

It is true that all sorts of miraculous things happened when we received Bibles: heavy downpours of rain, power cuts, secret police, and dogs put in a deep sleep. But now the foreign van was stuck there behind the church gates. And at six o'clock the secret police would start to patrol the street. They would notice it right away, and there would be trouble.

"Start the engine," I suggested. "We will pray that the Lord will keep everyone asleep."

Charlie started the engine, while the rest of us pushed hard.

The engine makes such a noise, I thought. *I am sure that woman across the street will wake up.*

She was paid to report to the secret police any move I made. She reported when I went out and when I came back. The neighbors up the street from the church were no better. They also had a big dog. But to my surprise nc lights came on. Charlie tried again and again to drive the camper forward and backward, but to no avail.

"I'll try to jack it up," he said.

The next we heard was a loud crack.

"The jack broke," Mary said.

Maybe the Lord allows us to go to prison for Him, I thought. *It is the end: interrogations, beatings, imprisonment in a cold cell....*

"We had better hide the Bibles," I suggested.

"Yes, let's," said Teodor. "Then at least we won't be caught with them."

"Follow me," I whispered. "I have a place to put them."

Each one took two bags full of Bibles and dragged them about fifty yards down the steep slope.

"There," I said, pointing to a big hole where we used to burn rubbish.

We put the bags there then walked back up the hill to get the next lot.

"I have never been so cold in all my life," Elena said, shivering.

"Me too," I mumbled. I was wearing two sweaters, a jacket, gloves, and boots—all the clothes I possessed. But still my hands were numb with cold and my lips were so frozen that I could hardly speak.

"It is three o'clock," Mary said as we finished.

"Now quickly cover the bags with soil," I said. "Then let's break some fir branches and take some logs from the wood pile to put on top."

With a garden fork he found in the shed behind the church, Teodor chipped away at the frozen ground to loosen the soil. I took a spade and covered the bags of Bibles with soil until they were hidden from view; Elena then spread some fir branches over the top. When we had finished, we went behind the church and had a talk together.

"When they come to get us," I said, "let's not breathe a word about the Bibles."

"What should we say?" Charlie asked.

"Let's say you came to visit us, we had a snack together, and then the van got stuck."

A feeling of resignation came over all of us. We were so cold and tired. Suddenly the Lord put a word into my mind: *Don't give up! Fight!*

"What else could we do to get out of here?" I asked.

"If only we had a stronger jack," Charlie replied.

"Wait here." I motioned them to stay. Taking Teodor with me, I unlocked the church gate and went out. All was quiet. We went down the street five houses to a neighbor who I knew was a mechanic. I knocked at the door. He woke up and came out.

"Excuse us at this time of night, but we need two strong jacks."

In a few minutes he was back.

"Return them when you are finished," was all he said.

We went back to the church, and Charlie jacked up the camper on the right side. Then we put a plank underneath the wheels before letting it down. After a few minutes, the van was out of the yard and on its way, and the jacks were returned to their owner.

I locked the gate and went into the church with Teodor and Elena. We cast ourselves before the Lord in praise. It was still dark, the neighbors had slept through all the noise, and by six o'clock the snow had covered all traces of the night's activities.

We were free and the Bibles were safe.

Veronica listened to my story in awe.

"How wonderful," she exclaimed. "The Lord was so good to you."

I joined hands with her and prayed, "Lord, please do a miracle again for my family."

Chapter Five

A Good Shepherd

It was April 1985, and President Ceauşescu was leading a war against the Bible. My family was at the top of the wanted list because of their underground work. "Get the Sfatcus," he ordered. "They should all be put in chains."

Iulian was a Sfatcu and he wondered, *Will they arrest me too?*

There was tension in town, and fear seized the whole church. Many had hidden away their Bibles. Even the word *Bibles* sent fear into people's hearts. Police were everywhere, searching homes for Christian literature and preventing people from gathering for evening prayer. Telephone lines were cut, the mail was stopped, and communication between believers was almost impossible. There were arrests, beatings, and interrogations.

Iulian, though only fifteen, was in the middle of it. Two of his uncles and their wives were under arrest. Six hundred Bibles had been confiscated from their hands. Iulian knew a lot about the underground work.

"You should never say a word about it," they taught him. And he never did.

He was a small boy for his age, but he looked so mature. His beautiful curly brown hair, deep brown eyes, and slightly pointed nose made him look like a musician. He was, but there was no time to play the flute or guitar now. He'd inherited humor from his grandfather, and that, together with his courage, often got him out of trouble. He remembered how his grandfather used to say, "The Lord is always with you, so be strong."

Today, his grandmother, who had raised him and his sister, Corina, took him aside and whispered in his ear, "Go to Rădăuți, to Uncle Avram. He has to have this message." She handed him a cassette.

Iulian put the cassette under his shirt, grabbed some money from a drawer, and set off. He walked fast on Strada Coşbuc, his hands in his pockets, kicking little stones on his way, trying to pretend he was relaxed. Inside, though, he was painfully alert. *Help me, Lord! Help me, Lord!* he repeated in his heart.

Since the time he was eight he used to be sent out to walk this distance, almost a mile, with the order, "Go and see what's going on." He would go and observe everything: cars waiting for no reason, men with dark glasses hiding behind telegraph poles, curtains moving strangely at windows with watching shadows behind them. He would bring back the most accurate report. If it was safe, the Bibles were brought in a van and unloaded in the dark in their underground cellar. From there they were distributed with much care.

Help me, Lord, to get the message to our contacts, Iulian prayed. *If they don't get this cassette, they will make the wrong move.* He did not look back at all. But his ears were very attentive. He heard steady footsteps behind him. They sounded like the boots of a soldier. *Am I being followed?* He quickened his step to catch a tram that was just pulling in. The steps behind him hurried too. He bought a ticket at the back door of the tram then he made his way through the crowd toward the front door of the wagon, ready to jump out if necessary.

I have to deliver it or destroy it, he thought. The tram was heading toward the center of town, close to the train station. Iulian looked through the window and saw many girls and boys his age laughing and playing happily. How different his life was from theirs!

In a few minutes the tram was there. Iulian jumped off and ran toward the station. He heard the same boots running behind him. He ran faster, and the boots ran faster too. Now he was sure he was being followed. There was no time to waste. He dashed into the station restroom, locked himself inside, took the cassette from under his shirt, threw it on the floor and crushed it under his heels. Then he flushed everything down the toilet. Taking a quick look to make sure that no trace was left, he came out. It had taken him less than a minute.

"So there you are," said the man, puffing and panting, as he arrived. Iulian looked for the first time into the face of his pursuer. He was a heavy man in his fifties, with a revolver at his side. "Why did you run like that?" the man demanded, his rough hands thoroughly searching Iulian's body. But he didn't find anything and Iulian returned home.

"I couldn't do it," he told his grandmother with tears in his eyes.

"At least it did not fall into their hands," she said. "Maybe God will give us another chance."

That same evening Iulian tried again with another copy of the message. This time he took his sister, Corina, with him. They took a suitcase full of clothes, hiding the cassette in the middle.

"Let's go," Iulian said. With their grandmother's silent prayer over them, they left. It was pitch dark. Corina was a year older than Iulian, and she'd had many adventures because of her faith. It was raining now and the wind whipped the leaves and branches. When they arrived at the wooded area of the street, someone appeared from behind a tree.

"Stop! Don't move."

A strong light shone into their eyes and on their suitcase. It was a policeman.

"What have you got in there?" he asked, pointing to the suitcase.

A moment of silence followed. Iulian thought everything was lost. His heart pounded. Suddenly he knew there was only one thing to try.

"Bibles!" he replied and started to laugh.

Corina joined him.

"Are you joking with me?" the policeman shouted, and then he started to curse. "Get out of my sight, crazy kids."

And that is exactly what they did. At midnight they arrived at their destination and delivered the message. The work with Bibles was protected.

On Monday, April 22, the prosecutor called Teodor and Erzsu for interrogation. They arrived at the secret police headquarters, and an officer took them into a room. They sat down on a wooden bench on the left. On the right was a desk with two chairs. The windows looked out onto Strada Sărărie. A slogan in red letters covered the wall behind the desk: *Trăiască Partidul Comunist Român și Fiul prea iubit, Nicolae Ceaușescu, aducătorul de fericire!* (Long Live the Romanian Communist Party and its Beloved Son, Nicolae Ceaușescu, Bringer of Happiness).

Teodor wore a gray suit and tie, a white shirt, and his best shoes. His light brown, slightly curly hair was parted on the left. Erzso, nervous but dignified in her brown corduroy dress and high-heeled shoes, sat close to her husband. Her brown eyes looked sad and tired.

The prosecutor entered the room with some papers in his hand. He had a large round face and glasses and wore a smart navy suit. He sat down at the desk, with a superior look on his face.

"I called you here to sign a declaration that you were in the car with Constantin Sfatcu on the night of April 19," he told them, shoving the papers across his desk. "Sign here."

Teodor took the declaration and read it. Erzso leaned over and read it too.

"I refuse to sign," Teodor said, his face pale.

"I will not sign either," said Erzso.

"Do you think we are so stupid? We know what happened that night." Then the prosecutor stood up and shouted, "We know you both ran away. I will prove it to you."

Lord, help us! Teodor prayed. He squeezed Erzso's hand to encourage her.

"On the evening of April 15, two foreigners came to your apartment," the prosecutor said as he paced the floor. "You were in the dining room. You took them into the kitchen, 'a safer place to talk' as you called it. They said they brought Bibles. You asked, 'How many? How big is your van? Is it left- or right-hand drive? Is the side door on the right?' Then you told them to drive forward into the yard of your pastor's house and that you would wait for them there. On the evening of April 19, you loaded the car with Bibles. Iosif Morcan and Radu Buliga were also there. Then you, your wife, and your brother drove off. Later that night, the police stopped your car. You both got out and ran away. This is the truth. You have to sign."

Teodor sat there and thought, *Yes, they know everything, but still I will not sign. If I go to prison too, who will fight for Costică?*

"I refuse to sign," he said.

Lord, You helped us to escape that night, Erzso prayed. *It is our first year of marriage and we were so happy.*

"I refuse," she said.

Other secret police officers came in to help the prosecutor. They shouted at Teodor and Erzso, threatened them, and interrogated them for hours, but Teodor and Erzso remained strong.

"So you do not want to sign," the prosecutor said finally, his round face flushed with frustration. "I will find plenty of witnesses against you."

At least, that is what he thought....

Teodor and Erzso walked home hand in hand. "Lord, protect us from evil men," they prayed.

The next day the secret police summoned Pastor Iosif Morcan. About forty years old, he had helped us distribute many Bibles in Romania. When he said good-bye to his wife and little daughter, his face was as peaceful as always. Then he walked up the hill from his house on Strada Şipoţel to the secret police headquarters.

Who knows whether I will ever see them again? he thought. *Give me wisdom on the spot as You promised,* he prayed. *Your Word says, "Do not worry about what to say or how to say it. At that time you will be given what to say, for it will not be you speaking, but the Spirit of your Father speaking through you"* (Matthew 10:19–20).

An officer took Iosif to the same office where Teodor and Erzso had been interrogated the day before.

"Sign this declaration that on the night of April 19, Dr. Teodor Sfatcu and his wife left in your car with Constantin Sfatcu," the prosecutor said.

"I refuse."

"We can demonstrate to you that every word you said and everything you did in the last ten days is known to us," the prosecutor continued. "Last Monday evening the foreigners who brought the Bibles gave you some gifts. They gave you a suit, your wife some coffee, and your little girl a dress. Your wife was afraid to have Bibles in the shed behind the house and urged you to move them. Then you lent your white Dacia to the Sfatcus so that they could transport the Bibles. That evening you helped them load the car. Dr. Sfatcu, his wife, and Constantin Sfatcu drove off in your car that night. Is that correct?"

Iosif remained silent.

"Aren't you a pastor, a servant of God, called to speak the truth?" the prosecutor persisted.

"Yes, I am."

"Then why do you refuse to make the declaration?"

"I am a shepherd called by God to give my life for the sheep, not to take their lives. I will not sign."

"You will pay for that," the prosecutor shouted. "Go home now!"

The next morning the prosecutor summoned Radu Buliga, a young brother in the church.

"Sign this declaration that on the night of April 19 you saw Dr. Teodor Sfatcu and his wife and Constantin Sfatcu together in the pastor's car," the prosecutor said. "We know you helped them load the car with Bibles."

"I will not sign."

"If you do not sign, your wife will be sent to work at the other end of the country. You will never see her again."

Radu was newly married and loved his wife, but he also loved the Lord.

"I will not sign," he said.

The prosecutor next called a police officer and said, "We saw Teodor Sfatcu's neighbor, an Orthodox Christian, outside in the yard that night, and he waved at the Sfatcus. Go to him and make him sign the declaration. We have to get some witnesses."

The police officer went to the neighbor and tried his best to get a declaration, but returned with nothing.

"'I don't want to sign anything against my neighbor,' the Orthodox man said. 'Dr. Sfatcu is a good man. He helped me when I was sick.'"

"So no one wants to sign. Then I will play another game," the prosecutor said with a sadistic smile on his face.

The next day he summoned Teodor, Erzso, and Pastor Iosif at the same time to a room at the Securitate headquarters. The three of them waited there for some time, not knowing what was in store for them.

Suddenly the door opened and two guards brought Costică in. His hands were handcuffed behind his back. One of the guards ordered him to walk across the room and to face the back wall. He was pale with black marks around his eyes, and terror was stamped on his face. His body shook, and his knees knocked uncontrollably.

"Is it true that Dr. Sfatcu and his wife were in the car with you?" the prosecutor asked Costică.

"Yes," he answered with a tremble in his voice.

"Did we force you to make this statement?" the prosecutor asked.

"No," replied Costică.

Erzso cried out, "He looks so changed. What did you do to him?"

"Do you think this is a health resort?" the prosecutor mocked.

Teodor, shocked at the sight of his brother, managed to say, "Take courage, Costică."

"Many are praying for you," added Pastor Iosif. He felt as if his heart was pierced with a sword.

The prosecutor had a victorious smile on his face as the guards led Costică away.

"Now you have to sign," he said confidently.

"I will not sign," said Teodor.

"Neither will I," said Erzso.

"I will not sign anything," said Pastor Iosif.

At this point the prosecutor dismissed them. "I will get you on other charges," he said as they walked out.

The plan would be to accuse Costică of attempted murder. If the police could prove that Teodor and Erzso were with him and ran away, then they could be arrested for complicity in the crime and also accused of trying to escape.

Proselytism was the next charge they attempted to bring against Teodor. The police searched their neighbor's house and found a Bible.

"Where did you get this?"

"I don't remember," the man answered.

"Didn't Dr. Sfatcu give it to you? Did he preach to you?"

"No."

The man understood that proselytism meant prison.

Denigrating the country was their next attempt. Teodor's telephone line was cut. One evening he went to the house of some friends. He spoke from their phone with friends in the United States.

"Costică has been caught with Bibles and is in prison."

The secret police listened in to the conversation and in half an hour they were there.

"Dr. Sfatcu denigrated the country abroad from your phone. You heard him say 'Constantin is in prison for Bibles,' but that is not true. No one is put in prison for Bibles in our country. We have freedom of religion in Romania. You have to sign a declaration that he denigrated the country."

"I did not hear what he said," the man replied.

"And I was with the children," his wife added.

"If you do not sign, you both will lose your jobs," the secret police said.

They refused.

Manslaughter was their next attempt. Teodor was a family doctor in Podu Iloaie, a village near Iaşi. The clinic where he worked was very poor, and most of his patients were gypsies. He worked hard and with love, often paying out of his own pocket for the medicines he prescribed. It was a time when infant mortality was high and lack of medicines brought many to a sudden death. The secret police watched Teodor hour by hour, day by day, for two months. They were sure that a patient or a baby would die, as often happened. They were well prepared to arrest him. But to everyone's astonishment, no one died in his hands for weeks on end.

During this period, Teodor's nurse came under such pressure, seeing so many secret police around, that she lost twenty pounds.

Demoralization was another tactic used by the secret police. At the time, Erzso went every day with Teodor to work. The secret police paid people to mock them. Every day a man would pass by his clinic and shout, "Ha! Ha! Where is your God? Why doesn't he save your brother, Constantin?" And at other times a woman would stop in front of the clinic and shout, "Is Dr. Sfatcu still free? Hasn't he been arrested yet? People like him should be in prison."

During all this time the church prayed and fasted around the clock for them.

One day a gypsy man came to Teodor with one of his many children. He tried hard to pronounce his name, Dr. Sfatcu, as he was a new doctor in the village. He repeated the name again and again, but when his turn came something else came out of his mouth.…

"Dr. Spartacus," he said. "My boy cannot breathe through his nose. He keeps his mouth open."

Teodor checked the boy, then turned to the father and explained, "Your son has sinusitis, an infection of the sinuses. Here is a prescription and some money to pay for it."

"Sinusitis. Sinusitis? Now, where did my son get this sickness from?" the gypsy man wondered. "This sickness must come from Syria."

Teodor laughed a lot.

Another time a woman from the village came with a very bad cough. Teodor gave her a bottle of cough mixture.

"Take a spoonful every day," he told her.

The next morning she came back with an empty bottle.

"Doctor, can you give me another bottle?" she said. "It tasted so good! And it softened my throat so well."

"So did you drink the whole bottle?" Teodor asked. "Here is another bottle, but just take one spoonful a day."

The patients loved Teodor, and the secret police had no success against him. The Lord watched over him and protected him.

Genovieva with a neighbor in front of the Sfatcu family
house on Str. Coşbuc, Iaşi, March 1980

Elena and Silvia
from Romania (left)
with Gaenor and Tricia
from Wales, 1985

Genovieva (center),
Silvia, and Dănuţ
(with guitars) at a
home meeting in
Iaşi, 1973

Chapter Six

The Torture Chamber

Costică was asleep in his cell in the basement of the secret police headquarters in Iaşi. It was a small room with cement walls and floor and a toilet in the corner. A light bulb hung from the ceiling. The narrow iron bed had a thin mattress, a sheet, and a musty, threadbare gray blanket.

Someone knocked at the door. "Wake up."

He opened his eyes and jumped out of bed.

The door opened and a soldier handed him a tray. On it was a piece of black bread and a cup of sweet tea.

He took it and ate and drank quickly. *Thank you, Lord. I was so hungry.*

Many questions passed through his mind. *Where are Estera and the children? Are they in the next cell? What about the rest of the family?*

Suddenly he realized that his cell was situated right under a beautiful park that he had known since he was a child. He used to pass it every day on his way to Costache Negruzzi Boys' High School. He again passed that way when he was a student for four years at the Faculty of Mechanical Engineering. Mauve and pink lilacs bloomed in that park in April and spread their sweet fragrance. Peacocks strutted freely on the lawns under the trees. He used to stop to admire their blue, green, and gold tail feathers. Passers-by like him could hear cluck-cluck-cluck from far away.

Costică also remembered how our father told him, "What a beautiful park! But…underneath are cells and interrogation rooms. Many believers suffer there because of the Bible." "Lord, have mercy on them," he used to pray, his hands clasped and his eyes toward heaven. Now Costică himself was there.

The soldier led Costică to the interrogation room. It was on the second level underground. Before he even entered the room, he heard moans and screams, and horror gripped his heart. It was a huge place with whitewashed walls and ceramic tiles on the floor. There were iron tables and instruments of torture everywhere. He saw innocent people being beaten and tortured in front of each other to make them sign false declarations of guilt.

The soldier showed Costică to a hard metal chair in front of one of the tables. "Sit down there," he said.

The torturers were big men like boxers. One of them had a big rubber stick on which was written: "SFÂRȘITUL LUMII" (THE END OF THE WORLD). He showed it to Costică and said with an evil smile, "Read what is written on my stick and beware."

Save me, Lord, Costică prayed silently.

A middle-aged, blue-eyed officer in a khaki uniform entered the room. He put his cap and a file on the table and sat down in a comfortable leather chair opposite Costică.

"I am Colonel Miron from Bucharest," he said. "I am part of the judicial commission set up for your case."

Lord, give me strength, Costică prayed. He shivered in his prisoner's clothes—a brown striped cotton suit and slippers.

Colonel Miron wrote the date on his paper: April 20, 1985. Then he leaned back in his chair.

"Mr. Sfatcu, you have to tell me everything. I want to inform you that your whole family is also under interrogation in another room."

These words pierced Costică's heart like a sword. *Lord, give me grace,* he prayed.

At that moment someone screamed in agony. Costică turned his head and saw a man tied to one of the tables being beaten on the soles of his feet. *Lord, have mercy on him.* Tears came to his eyes, and he started to cry.

"This is what they will do to you if you do not cooperate," said Miron with no emotion. "Do you suppose they will treat you any better?"

Costică trembled with fear.

"So let's talk about the Bibles," Miron continued. "Enemies brought them into the country," he said looking straight at Costică. "But we give you a chance to come over to our side."

A woman strapped facedown to another table was savagely beaten on her kidneys. "Sign! Sign!" they shouted. "I am not guilty! I am not guilty!" she screamed back. They beat her until she was unconscious.

Father, have mercy on her, Costică prayed.

Colonel Miron continued, "If you tell us all you know about Bibles, you can be free in a moment."

The torturer with the stick on which was written "THE END OF THE WORLD" walked straight toward Costică and swung the stick at him.

Terror filled Costică's heart. *Am I next?*

But the torturer walked away without touching him.

Colonel Miron made himself comfortable in his chair. He looked at Costică and asked, "Do you know someone by the name of Ulf Oldenburg?"

"Yes," Costică said. "He is from Denmark."

"Did he bring you Bibles?"

"He brought Bibles to my father many years ago."

"What year was that?"

"It was 1967."

"Where did your father hide those Bibles?"

"Well…in the attic…in the wardrobe…in the pantry."

Ulf had driven all the way to Romania in a Volkswagen bug. He hid the Bibles in the trunk. What joy those Bibles gave our father! Costică could still hear him say, "These books are pure gold."

"Where did your father take those Bibles?"

"I don't know. I was only fourteen."

"How many times did Mr. Oldenburg come with Bibles in his car?"

"Two or three times. I don't know."

"Do you know Tărniceriu Pricop?"

"Yes."

"Did your father take Bibles to him?"

"I saw him give him some. I don't know how many."

"What about Ursan from Vânători?"

"He gave him some too."

In fact, Costică knew that over the years, our father had taken many hundreds of Bibles to these contacts.

"What about Andriciuc?"

"I think my father took him some."

Costică knew that this old pastor was one of the key contacts in the village of Vânători. He also knew that he had a storage place in his goat shed and that he had received hundreds of Bibles.

They want to find out about our distribution network, Costică thought.

"How many missions do you know from Holland?" Colonel Miron asked.

"None."

"Do you know the organization, Open Doors?"

"No."

"Do you know Brother Andrew?"

"No."

"Open Doors is an illegal organization that smuggles Bibles into our country. What would the Dutch secret police say if we smuggled weapons or pornography into Holland? Well, Bibles are just as dangerous."

Colonel Miron put his feet on the table and went on, "Do you know Gaenor and Tricia, two girls from Great Britain?"

"Yes." Costică nodded.

"What are their family names?"

"I don't know."

"Do they work for Open Doors?"

"They never told me."

The soldier came back in and went straight to Miron. "Coffee and cheesecake are ready for you in the restaurant, Colonel," he said.

Miron got up, lit a cigarette, and swaggered from the room.

Costică remained in his chair. *Now they want to know about Gaenor and Tricia,* he thought. *What are they after?*

These two missionaries had come to Romania with Bibles and they'd told him a story about how they'd protected the Bibles with Welsh cookies....

Gaenor and Tricia had crossed the border with Bibles hidden in their camping van. They needed to find a place to open the secret compartments and unload. They found a rest area with a picnic table beside a forest. It was a safe spot. At least, they thought so....

"I will take the stove outside and prepare the meal," Gaenor said. "That way I can keep watch while you unload the Bibles."

"Yes, that's a good idea," Tricia agreed.

Gaenor and Tricia were from Wales and they spoke Welsh together.

"If the police come, I will shout," Gaenor continued. "They won't understand a word of Welsh."

Tricia went inside the van and drew the curtains. She pressed a hidden button under the dash, and the secret compartments opened. It was hard work to get the Bibles out and put them into thick, black garbage bags. She tied them up securely ready for delivery: almost one thousand Bibles.

Outside the van, Gaenor opened a can of concentrated, creamy soup. She poured it into a pot and mixed it with water. Then she lit the camping stove. While waiting for the soup to boil, she laid the table, opened a tin of cookies, and poured orange juice into two cups. The pot on the stove started to boil and spread the inviting aroma of chicken and pea soup. The birds were singing in the trees and everything around seemed peaceful.

Suddenly Gaenor noticed a car approaching. She watched as it got nearer, turned into the rest area, and stopped right behind the van. Two policemen got out.

Gaenor immediately shouted as loud as she could in Welsh the word for danger: "*Perygl! Perygl!*" She tried to keep a smile on her face.

"What danger?" one of the policemen asked in English.

"Oh, there is no danger," Gaenor answered, gesturing to the stove. "I was just talking to my friend in Welsh—the soup is ready."

Tricia quickly covered the Bibles with blankets and got out of the van.

"We heard you say, '*Pericol! Pericol,*' which means *danger* in Romanian," the other policeman said.

"We were speaking Welsh, not Romanian," Gaenor explained calmly.

"Please have some delicious cookies from Wales," Tricia said.

The policemen took as many as they could in their hands and walked away laughing and repeating, "Pericol! Pericol!"

They were almost caught, but the Lord saved them! Costică thought. *Will the Lord save me too?*

The clock in the hall struck eleven.

Colonel Miron came back after his coffee break, sat down again in his chair, and resumed the interrogation.

"How many missions from Austria brought Bibles to your family?"

"Maybe two or three," Costică said.

"How did these missions transport the Bibles?"

"In their cars."

In another corner, a torturer was beating a man's hands. They were swollen to double the normal size, and he was moaning piteously.

Lord, unless You help me, I have no strength to go through this, Costică prayed.

"We have all sorts of ways to make you talk," Miron threatened. "Now let's get to the last transport of Bibles. Do you know Stephen Beattie from England?"

"Yes," said Costică.

"Why did he come to see you last month?"

"He is a friend of our family."

"Did he send you this last transport of Bibles?"

Stephen had arranged the transport, but did not bring the Bibles himself.

"No."

"How did these Bibles get through the border?"

Costică was glad he didn't know how the Bibles got into the country.

"I don't know," he replied.

In another corner of the room, the torturer with the rubber stick was beating a doctor over his head. "So, you plotted against the government!"

"No I didn't," the doctor replied, not even cringing under the blows. His voice was dull and lifeless. Costică looked at the doctor and knew that he was going out of his mind.

"We will do the same to you if you do not cooperate," Miron reminded Costică. "Did you also receive Russian Bibles?"

"No."

"With whom did you work in Moldova?"

"I don't know anyone there."

When evening came, Colonel Miron wrote a report of the day's interrogation, picked up Costică's file, and left for the day.

The first day of Costică's interrogation was over.

For the next three months he was asked the same questions in that terrible place. Every day a different officer came to question him from morning till evening. Every day he was interrogated in different ways about Bibles. And every day he saw and heard other prisoners being tortured.

One day, after three months, Colonel Miron brought Costică a typed paper.

"Read this and sign," he said.

Costică read it silently: "Declaration: I, Sfatcu Constantin, declare that on the evening of April 19, 1985, I attempted to murder a policeman who stopped me in the street. I confess that I am guilty and sign my name."

How incredible, he thought to himself. *They interrogated me only about Bibles for three months and now they accuse me of attempted murder. But I know what they will do to me in this place if I refuse to sign.* Suddenly he knew what to do. *I will sign it*, he thought. *It is the only way I can live and not die.*

He signed the declaration and handed it to Colonel Miron, who seemed well pleased.

"Thank you, Mr. Sfatcu," he said and left with a smile.

The soldier came and took Costică back to his cell. He lay down on the hard iron bed. Then he heard the Holy Spirit whisper to him words from Isaiah 43: "Fear not, for I have redeemed you; I have summoned you by name; you are mine. When you pass through the waters, I will be with you; and when you pass through the rivers, they will not sweep over you. When you walk through the fire, you will not be burned."

With these words he fell asleep.

Chapter Seven

The Day of the Trial

It was June 1985. I was in the United States when I received news that the date of Costică's trial was set. An overwhelming sadness came over me. I wept as if I had to be ready for a funeral. President Ceaușescu's order to destroy my family seemed impossible to overthrow. I read in the Bible, "Be faithful, even to the point of death, and I will give you the crown of life" (Revelation 2:10). Would the Lord allow my family to die?

During this time I stayed with my old friend Veronica Sușman in Ohio. That summer the immigration office in Cleveland called me for my citizenship examination. I had to read books about American history to prepare myself. It was good to have this study to occupy me at this difficult time in my life.

It was a sunny spring morning and the sky was blue. I sat in the garden on the bench under the cherry tree. I watched the sparrows feed their young in the bird box. Veronica brought two cups of cherry compote and sat down next to me.

I missed my family so much, and it helped to share my memories of them with Veronica. Today I chose the story of how God used a box of Bibles in our own house.

One night my family received Bibles. Costică, Teodor, and my friend Silvia were with me. The Bibles came in boxes of fifty, and we put them in the front room on the wooden floor. In this room was a bed with a hay mattress, which Teodor and I filled with sweet-smelling dry grass every year. Next to the door was a wardrobe, and opposite the window was our bookcase.

A friend of my father's came that night, and we loaded the boxes into his car. He took them to a hiding place in a village.

After we finished, we all fell asleep on the bed. The night was not long, but we slept well because we were tired. My parents and Corina and Iulian slept in the back room.

Early the next morning, the roosters woke us up: Cock-a-doodle-doo! My mother went out to feed the chickens and geese.

Before he went to work, my father asked in a whisper, "Did all the boxes go?"

"Yes," I said. But I was wrong....

"May the Lord protect the Bibles and us all," he said as he left.

"Breakfast is ready," Mama called from the kitchen. She served us coffee with milk, fresh bread and homemade plum jam.

We hardly finished eating when we heard the dogs bark, then a knock at the door. Two men were there. The first one was a short, brusque man in his forties: Colonel Aldea from the secret police. His eyes glinted an icy blue, and even his reddish, curly hair was not permitted to be free but was instead brushed backward in a harsh style. The other man was a police officer in uniform.

"We have a search warrant," Aldea said and showed us a piece of paper.

They entered the house and came straight into the front room.

"Identification papers please," said the officer. He checked our papers and put them aside.

"Stand in that corner," he ordered us. "Don't move and don't touch anything."

How good that we got the Bibles out last night! I thought.

Aldea searched every room in the house, while the officer guarded us. I heard the clink of plates and knew he was opening cupboards in the kitchen. His footsteps went from there into the pantry. I could tell when he put the ladder up against the wall to open the attic door. Later I heard the familiar squeak of the old wooden wardrobe from Bohemia, and I knew he was searching my parents' room.

After half an hour he came back in the front room. He checked quickly under the hay mattress and in the wardrobe.

Suddenly fear gripped me. I could not believe what I saw—a box of Bibles! It sat in plain view next to the wardrobe. I felt my heart beat fast.

How did we forget that box? I wondered. I glanced at the others, and I saw that they noticed it too.

Lord, blind their eyes, I prayed.

Then…Aldea rushed straight toward the box of Bibles. He pushed it with his foot toward the bookcase.

We are finished, I thought.

"I want to have a look up there," he said and pointed to the top of the bookcase. Then, to our astonishment, he stepped on the box of Bibles in order to reach up. But all he found there were a few empty instrument cases and a layer of dust. He stepped down again and went out to wash his hands.

Then he looked at his watch and said to his colleague, "It's late. Let's go."

And they left in their car.

"I will never forget what the Lord did for us, Veronica," I concluded.

"What a wonderful miracle!" she said. "God can do anything, Genovieva."

I prayed again that He would protect my family during Costică's trial.

———————

The day of the trial came, June 27, 1985. Early in the morning all my family went to the courthouse in Iași. It was a gray, two-story building in the center of the city, surrounded by a brick wall and old oak trees. Many friends from different churches were there already, waiting for the doors to open. They all came to attend the trial as a sign of love and solidarity with my family. Two officials from the American Embassy promised to come as well.

Teodor, holding his wife by the hand, looked among the crowd, hoping to see them somewhere. He saw our sister, Aurora, talking to two strangers. *Are they the Americans from the Embassy?* he wondered. He made his way to them at once.

"Oh, Teodor, I looked everywhere for you," said Aurora in English, taking him by the sleeve. "I talked to Smith and Mary from the American Embassy. They told me you met them already."

"No, I didn't. Thank you so much for coming," he said as he shook hands with them.

"Glad to be here," Mary answered.

"We came to show solidarity with you," said Smith.

"But Teodor," interrupted Aurora, "They told me you met them earlier this morning. Didn't you?"

"No," Teodor repeated. "This is the first time we met."

"Are you Teodor Sfatcu, brother of Constantin?" asked Smith with a puzzled expression.

"Yes, of course," Teodor replied.

"Well, let me explain what happened," said Smith. "We arrived last night by train and checked in at the Unirea Hotel. This morning after breakfast, as we came out of the hotel, a man that looked like you stopped us and asked, 'Are you from the American Embassy?' 'Yes,' we replied. 'I am Teodor Sfatcu,' he said, 'brother of Constantin. I'm sorry to tell you that the trial was postponed. It will not take place today. You should return to Bucharest and come back on the right day.'"

"Then I suggested we walk to the courthouse anyway," Mary joined in. "And I am so glad we did. Your sister saw us, knew we were foreigners, and came to speak to us."

"Incredible," Teodor said and nodded in understanding. "And by the way, I am the real Teodor Sfatcu and this is my wife, Erzso. The trial is not postponed—in fact I have just read the list on the window, and Constantin is the first to be tried. Let's go in right away."

They went in and looked for seats. The court was packed. Soon the gong sounded and the clerk called the name of the accused: "Sfatcu Constantin!" The crowd waited in silence. Then the clerk called again: "Sfatcu Constantin!" After a few moments he announced, "The accused, Sfatcu Constantin, did not come for the trial. The trial is postponed."

An officer asked the crowd to leave the hall immediately, so that the next case could begin.

"What a surprise…and a blow," Teodor said. "Especially because many came from far away."

The crowd dispersed quickly.

"The judge did not want to try Costică in front of you," Aurora explained to Smith and Mary.

"They postponed the trial because they could not deceive you," Teodor added.

Teodor, Erzso, Aurora, and their foreign guests walked slowly to the car. Teodor held the car keys in his hand, ready to open the door, when another surprise met his eyes.

"Look at that," he said, pointing. "Someone slashed all the tires."

"The secret police," said Erzso.

"We will walk home," said Teodor. "Mama prepared lunch."

They walked together up the hill of Copou toward Mama's house. All the way, the lime trees gave them shade and spread their sweet perfume. As they went, Teodor shared with the guests how the police had caught them with Bibles and how he and Erzso escaped. They also shared their fear that the police would arrest them too.

"Where is Constantin's wife, Estera?" Mary asked.

"She was there in the crowd with her mother and the children," Teodor explained. "She has many guests of her own—many friends and relatives who came for the trial. She sends her love to you and is very thankful that you came."

When they arrived, Mama welcomed them with a smile. The table was set with a white tablecloth and her best earthenware dinner service. In the middle of the table was a vase of red geraniums. She served them borscht with dill and parsley, stuffed cabbage, and fresh bread. For dessert she gave them confiture made from bitter cherries. Everyone enjoyed her cooking.

"We will come back when the trial takes place," Smith promised the family. That encouraged them.

Later that afternoon my family accompanied the Americans to the station, and they left on the train back to Bucharest.

From Veronica's home in Ohio, I kept in close touch with my family in Iaşi. When I heard the news that the trial was postponed, I was distressed, not knowing what would happen. I needed all the encouragement I could get.

Richard Wurmbrand, who had spent fourteen years in prison for his faith, called me often, and he and his wife, Sabina, encouraged me in the Lord. "We will publicize the situation," he said.

"We are praying for you," Sabina added.

Senator Huff from Kentucky also called me to ask how the trial went. He sensed my distress and read some verses from the Bible to me over the phone: "Because he loves me," says the LORD, "I will rescue him; I will protect him, for he acknowledges my name. He will call upon me, and I will answer him; I will be with him in trouble, I will deliver him and honor him" (Psalm 91:14–15).

Oh, how much these verses lifted my spirits!

Chapter Eight

At the Courthouse

It was July 1985 and I feared the worst for my family, because they had been caught with Bibles. I was still far away from them, in the United States, waiting for my appointment with the Immigration and Naturalization Service. I kept in close touch with the situation in Romania by phone.

––––––––––

The day of the trial in Iași was rescheduled for July 11. Early that sunny morning, many people gathered in front of the gray stone courthouse building. Each one of them hoped to get a seat when the doors opened. Two representatives from the American Embassy, Paul Urly and Scott Edelman, were also present.

Half an hour before the trial, a police officer came and addressed the crowd in the yard. He wore a navy blue uniform with shiny boots.

"Those who came for Sfatcu's case, come up here," he said through a microphone as he motioned with his hand.

About two hundred people stepped up and crowded around him at the front door. The others stepped back under the shade of some old oak trees. They were there out of curiosity to attend a trial for Bibles.

However, Teodor noticed that many who were neither family nor friends of the family joined his group at the front. *Secret police*, he thought.

Another officer opened a window on the second floor of the courthouse.

"You are too many here. Only the family is allowed in," he shouted to the crowd below. "The rest of you, get away from the door. Go home."

"Why? Why?" the crowd murmured in disappointment.

"Only the family is allowed in. The rest go home."

"Let us all in. Let us all in! We are all family—the family of God," the infiltrators shouted, shaking their fists and pushing forward.

"Don't push, don't push!" the women and children screamed, caught in the middle. "We cannot breathe. Help! Help!"

"Let us all in," the infiltrators continued to shout as they pushed.

"Order. Order!" the police officer shouted from the window.

"This is how believers behave—like hooligans," another officer said.

In the middle of this well-staged chaos, Teodor noticed two muscular policemen next to him who looked like boxers. He overheard one of them say to the other, "Now, get the Americans!"

While one made room behind him, the other one turned and punched Scott Edelman in the stomach as hard as he could.

"Yow!" Scott winced at the sudden blow, but kept his calm.

However, when the policeman swung his fist to strike Paul Urly, his watch flew off.

"My watch! My watch," he shouted. He pushed everyone aside and stooped down to look for it. But all he found was broken pieces.

A young man saw what happened. He heard the Holy Spirit whisper, "Go and buy him a watch." He hurried to a nearby department store and came back with the best watch he could find.

"Please accept this as a gift. I am sorry for what happened," he said.

"Oh—thank you," replied the policeman. He stepped aside, thoughtful…and put on his new watch.

Ding, dong. Ding, dong. The big clock in the city struck nine. The doors of the courthouse opened. Hundreds of people scrambled to enter the hall. They took their seats in silence.

From his front seat Teodor stood up and looked around. The hall was packed.

Where is Dănuţ? he wondered. *It is strange that he is not here. He promised to come.*

Dănuţ was a young brother in the church and a close friend of the family. He spoke good English and was a keen observer. The secret police did not want him at the trial.

When he arrived at work that morning, he went to his boss. "I need to take today off. I have an important meeting."

"No problem," his boss said. "But first, come with me upstairs."

Dănuţ followed him to the second floor, unsuspecting.…

The boss opened a door. Dănuţ recognized it as the room used by the security guard. He took a quick look around and saw a narrow bed, some armchairs, and a little table in the middle. There was a bathroom and a kitchen corner with a coffee machine. Heavy curtains covered the window.

"Sit down here," the boss said and offered him a soft chair.

Dănuţ made himself comfortable. He smelled the aroma of freshly ground coffee.

The boss opened the refrigerator. He got out milk and some apple pastries and put them on the table.

"I have something to tell you," his boss said as he poured two cups of coffee.

Why such treatment? Dănuţ wondered. *Besides, it is nine o'clock and I should be at the courthouse.*

At that moment the telephone rang. The boss answered.

"Okay, okay. I will come down."

Then he turned to Dănuţ. "Excuse me just a moment. I will be right back."

Dănuţ nodded and his boss left the room, closing the door behind him. *Click-click.*

What did I hear? Did he lock me in? He jumped up and tried the door. He pulled at the handle from the inside and knocked with his fists.

"Let me out! Let me out!" he shouted, but it was too late.

He ran to the window and drew the curtains aside.

The window was barred. *No way to get out. I am trapped. Lord, what should I do?*

The Holy Spirit brought some verses to his mind, and he recited them: "'May God arise, may his enemies be scattered; may his foes flee before him. As smoke is blown away by the wind, may you blow them away; as wax melts before the fire, may the wicked perish before God. But may the righteous be glad and rejoice before God; may they be happy and joyful…' (Psalm 68:1–3). Father, I claim these wonderful promises for Costică and the Sfatcu family right now," he prayed.

All that day, locked in that room, Dănuţ interceded for his brothers.

Finally, back at the courthouse, the accused, Sfatcu Constantin, was brought in through a side door. All heads turned toward him. He was chained and handcuffed. His head was shaved, and he wore striped prison clothes.

"Oh, oh…!" Muffled exclamations came from the awestruck crowd.

Then, complete silence. Costică stood in the dock, the judges and lawyers on one side and the public on the other side. He looked around and caught a glimpse of his family and friends from the church.

A gong sounded and the trial started. The prosecutor, dressed in a black suit and tie, stood up and read the charges.

"On the evening of April 19, 1985, at about ten o'clock, the accused, Sfatcu Constantin, was stopped in a routine police check. The police officer asked to see in the back of the car. The accused pretended to take the keys from the ignition, but instead started the engine again and tried to drive away. The officer, holding the steering wheel, tried to take the keys out of the ignition. In the fight that followed, the car covered a distance of approximately thirty meters at a speed of about thirty kilometers per hour. The police officer was dragged along the pavement and in this way his life was put in danger. Sfatcu Constantin is accused of the premeditated attempted murder of a high state official."

Then it was the turn of the witness and the plaintiff.

"I saw the policeman being dragged along the pavement by the car," the taxi driver said. "There was a fight between him and the driver."

"This is what Sfatcu Constantin did to me in the fight," the policeman said, as he showed a scratch on his hand.

What lies, Costică thought. *Defend me, O Lord! There was no fight.*

Then the defense lawyer spoke. "I draw attention to the fact that the accusations are inconsistent. There is only flimsy evidence that the policeman was hurt at all."

The judge then asked Costică, "Do you have anything to say in your defense?"

"Since I was arrested three months ago, I was interrogated only about Bibles," he said, his body trembling violently. "I am surprised that you accuse me of attempted murder. I am not guilty." Tears streamed down his cheeks, but he couldn't use his hands to wipe them away.

Then the judge solemnly announced the verdict: "Guilty of malicious, premeditated attempted murder of a high state official."

There was a loud murmur in the audience.

As Costică was led out of the courthouse, he took a last look at his family. *Will I ever see them again?* he wondered.

A car was waiting for him and, surrounded by armed police, he got in. *Which prison will they take me to?* he wondered. *Lord, help me!*

After they drove for about five kilometers, the car stopped, and he was ordered out. It was not hard to recognize the place. It was the prison next to our family's house.

Toward evening Dănuț's boss returned, unlocked the door, and apologized. "Sorry about that," he said. "I only obeyed instructions."

Nine days later, in Costică's absence, an officer read the following sentence in a public hearing:

"...for these reasons, in the name of the law, it is decided: The accused, Sfatcu Constantin, son of Neculai and Maria, born April 4, 1953, resident in Iași, Strada Petru Rareș 5, married with two children, mechanical engineer, no previous convictions, held in custody at the police headquarters in

Iași, is sentenced for the crime of attempted murder according to article 20 with reference to articles 174 and 175 letter F of the penal code [articles referring to malicious, premeditated action against a high state official] to seven years and six months imprisonment and four years' loss of civil rights, according to article 64 letters A and B of the penal code [referring to rights to employment, medical and social benefits].... The accused is obliged to pay legal costs to the state of fourteen hundred *lei*.... Sentence pronounced in the public session of July 20, 1985."

When Costică was a child, he had heard terrifying screams coming from inside those walls. He saw prisoners pass by the family house in convoys to their place of work. He remembered how our father asked us children to sing, "God be with you till we meet again," as they went by. At the entrance to our street were signs in several languages, which read: "Forbidden to Foreigners."

Now the prison was rebuilt with three walls round the outside and underground cells. It held up to ten thousand prisoners. And one of them was Costică.

He soon learned to obey the discipline of the prison. A soldier led him to a large room that had iron bunk beds four high and assigned him a bed on level four. Fifty prisoners slept in that dormitory. There were only two washbasins and one toilet. There were always long lines to use these facilities.

The window was covered by a metal plate with small holes. Fresh air could hardly penetrate it, and the air in the cell was stuffy. The beds were covered with thin blankets infested with bed bugs. At night the bright fluorescent lights were never turned off.

At quarter past five a loud gong sounded, and Costică woke up with the other prisoners. Through a little window a guard handed each prisoner a tray of food with a chunk of bread and a cup of coffee.

For the last two or three years, Costică had suffered from stomach ulcers and colitis. He took medication and kept a strict diet that avoided many things, including dark bread and coffee. Any time he did not keep this diet, which had been advised by his doctor, he had immediate pain. *Lord, please bless this food and heal me*, he prayed, *I am so hungry.* Then he ate and drank quickly…and waited. *Thank You, Lord!* He had no pain.

All that morning he sang a song in his heart. It was a beautiful tune with words from Psalm 103: "Praise the LORD, O my soul…who forgives all your sins and heals all your diseases."

Lunch was served at half past two. Costică looked in his bowl: heavy, greasy soup with beans, potatoes and cabbage. *Lord, the doctor forbade me to eat such things*, he prayed, *but I am so hungry.* Then he ate it. No pain. *Thank You, Lord! How wonderful You are!*

The evening meal was at nine o'clock. It was a bowl of boiled wheat. He saw mice droppings, hair, and worms in the wheat, but he ate it anyway. He remembered the verse from Proverbs 27: "To the hungry even what is bitter tastes sweet."

As the weeks went by in that prison, Costică never had any more pain or problems with his stomach. He knew that the Lord healed him. It was an answer to his prayers, and to the prayers of many.

The believers in Iaşi prayed and fasted against the spirit of false witness. They did not know how the Lord would answer their prayers.

About a week after the trial, Estera's uncle and his wife came from Rădăuţi and took her out for a meal. The restaurant in Copou could seat about a hundred people. After they entered, they put on their trays chicken with garlic, green salad, fresh bread rolls, and mineral water with syrup. They looked around for a table, but all the tables were full. Soon a family stood up and left. A waitress cleaned the table for them and invited them to come.

They sat down and Uncle Avram prayed, "Thank You, Lord for the food. May Costică not be hungry in prison."

"And deliver him and Estera from evil men," Lidia continued.

"Amen," said Estera.

In the middle of their meal Estera said, "This is such a treat for me. The chicken is so delicious. At home I hardly—"

A look of shock came over her face.

"I can't believe my eyes!" she whispered. "Look…the prosecution witnesses." She motioned with her eyes to the next table.

The policeman who had stopped the car that night was there with his wife and cousin. With them was the taxi driver. There was a lot of food on their table and several empty bottles. They seemed drunk.

"Since I got involved with these believers…and their Bibles…I haven't had one good night's sleep," the police officer said.

"Why is that?" his cousin asked.

"I have nightmares that I stand before the throne of God. He is very angry with me. I see fire and brimstone." He clenched his fists on the table. "I take sleeping pills, but they don't help."

The taxi driver nodded. "It is the same with me. My conscience bothers me, and I feel afraid all the time. My wife tells me that I lost my sense of humor."

"I am going to change my declaration," said the police officer. "Really, Sfatcu did not hurt me. He just had Bibles, that's all. That night I received an order from the secret police, 'Get the Sfatcus or you will be shot.'"

"Yes, the secret police put the words in our mouths," said the taxi driver. "I was witness that night to the discovery of six hundred Bibles, but that was all."

They finished their meal with a bottle of *țuică,* Romanian whiskey. Arm in arm, leaning on each other, they stumbled out of the restaurant.

Estera and her relatives also got up to leave.

"Thank You, Lord, that You are at work," Estera said, a small smile on her face.

"That was incredible," Lidia said.

"Praise the Lord!" said Avram.

The three of them walked home arm in arm.

———————

My family told me on the phone about Costică's sentence. I cried a lot and couldn't eat.

A few days later I had my appointment at the Immigration and Naturalization Service in Cleveland, Ohio. That morning I put on my best blue velvet dress. A hairdresser did my short, brown hair with a fringe. I had to look special that day. I put on my favorite rose perfume. It was the day when I was to become an American citizen.

The INS center was a massive gray building. It was full of new immigrants who were to be sworn in that day as citizens. An officer asked me to answer a questionnaire and one of the questions was, "Have you ever been a member of the Communist Party?" I wrote in giant letters: "NO! NO! NO!"

It was a happy moment in my life, but there was so much sadness in my heart. My thoughts were with my family. I suddenly became so weak that I lay down on the carpet.

The kind officer who had interviewed me asked, "What is wrong? Are you sick?"

"No," I said. "I just received the news that my brother in Romania was sentenced to prison for Bibles, and my whole family is in big trouble."

"I am so sorry," he said. He brought me a cup of orange juice.

I drank it.

"Thank you," I said. "That gave me strength."

"Welcome to America," he said. Then he added, "It usually takes at least three weeks for certificates to be mailed, but I promise that you will be the first to receive it."

How much I needed that kindness! In a few days I received my naturalization certificate, dated July 26, 1985. And how many times I thanked the Lord for the United States!

Wedding of Stephen and Genovieva in Guildford, England,
November 16, 1985. In the front row are Maynard and Jessie Beattie
(left), and Maria Sfatcu (right). At the back are Senator Gene and Ethel
Huff, and Ruth and Mary Beattie (far right).

Costică and
Estera, just
married at the
registry office in
Iaşi, June 1976

Wedding of
Costică and Estera,
Iaşi, June 1976

Chapter Nine

"Will You Marry Me?"

In August 1985, after I received United States citizenship, I applied for a passport. During this time I stayed with my friend Veronica in her little house in Akron, Ohio.

"Genovieva, you cry too much," Veronica remarked one day as we were shelling peas on a bench in the garden.

"I cry because I have only bad news from Romania," I said. "All the time I think of Costică in prison. I worry what will happen to the rest of my family."

"Lord, give Genovieva some good news as well," she prayed.

One morning soon after that, the telephone rang in her home.

"It is for you, Genovieva," Veronica said. "It's Stephen…from Austria."

Stephen had kept in touch with me regularly, calling about once a week to encourage me regarding my family. I did not expect that it would be anything different this time.

"Hello, Genovieva!" he said as usual. "How are you?"

"Well…no good news yet about my family," I replied.

"There is a lot of publicity about Costică's case. Christian magazines all over the world have published articles about your family."

"I am so glad you tell me that. Publicity will certainly help."

"Did you get your citizenship?"

"Yes, and I applied for a passport."

"When are you coming back to Austria?" he asked

"I don't know. Why?"

"I miss you, Genovieva.… I love you."

"I love you too!"

"Will you come to marry me?"

"Wow! Yeee-sss!" I shouted down the phone.

I jumped up and down with the telephone in my hand and I shouted to Veronica, "I'm going to Austria to marry Stephen!" I roared with laughter.

Stephen waited until I quieted down, then asked, "So, when can you come?"

"As soon as I receive my passport, I will be on the next plane," I said.

"I'll be waiting for you!"

For the first time in months my heart was filled with joy and hope.

Senator Gene Huff also kept in close touch with me. He wanted news of my family so that he could pass it on to intercessors. He and his wife, Ethel, invited me to Kentucky again to speak in churches, to raise awareness of the suffering church. I traveled there by bus for a weekend.

Gene Huff was not only a senator, but also a pastor. He cared for me at that time as a shepherd cares for a wounded sheep.

One evening I sat on the deck with his family and ate barbecued chicken with them. I told them my happy news. "Stephen asked me to marry him."

"Oh, how exciting!" said Ethel. "You see, the Lord wants to bless you."

"Tell us about Stephen," Gene asked.

"He used to be a French teacher, but gave up his job to become a Bible smuggler," I replied. "The mission he works with smuggled one hundred seventy-five thousand of my children's books into Romania."

"Wow, he must be courageous!" Ethel commented.

"I joked with him one day, 'If you smuggle my children's books into Romania, I will marry you.' He replied, 'And if you learn to make English tea the proper way, I will marry you.' He smuggled the books and I learned to make the tea."

They all laughed.

"But I have a question," I said. "Do you think I have a right to be happy when my family is in trouble? Won't people think I am indifferent to their suffering?"

"Oh, no," Ethel said. "The Lord gives you a husband to help you through this hard time. A husband and wife strengthen each other."

"This is from the Lord," Gene said. "And if you need a father to give you away, I will be there."

Thank You, Lord, for blessing me, I said in my heart.

I would need a father to give me away. My father had died, poisoned by the secret police, while I was still living in Romania.

––––––––––––––––

The cell where Costică was held in Iași had thick walls and barred windows. The guards had to unlock three doors in order to get in. It was impossible to escape from there. In spite of that, they checked the bars and counted the prisoners twice a day, at seven in the morning and at seven in the evening.

Costică dreaded these roll calls. Every morning he heard a shout: "*Aapel! Fața la perete!*" (Roll call! Face to the wall!). He faced the wall with the other prisoners and stood there motionless and in silence for two hours. The same was repeated in the evening.

Why do I need to stand up for so long? Costică wondered. His legs were weak, and he felt dizzy. *This is just to cause us suffering.*

Then one morning he heard the Lord speak to him. "I want you to use this time to talk with Me."

From that time on, Costică turned the roll call into a time of prayer and praise. Some verses from Psalm 27 came to his mind: "Hear my voice when I call, O LORD; be merciful to me and answer me. My heart says of you, 'Seek his face!' Your face, LORD, I will seek. Do not hide your face from me, do not turn your servant away in anger; you have been my helper. Do not reject me or forsake me, O God my Savior."

Suddenly he felt free from any human plans, desires, or ambitions— free from sin and the world. It did not matter to him anymore whether he lived or died. "I only want to please You, Lord," he prayed.

One evening Costică noticed three other prisoners praying. They clasped their hands and turned their eyes toward heaven.

"Take courage," one of them said.

"Be strong," another one said.

There were other Christian prisoners with him in the same dormitory, men who were falsely charged with hooliganism. The police had caught them reading the Bible, praying, or singing to the Lord in a home meeting.

The Christians in the dormitory had to be careful not to complain. There were informers among them. If one said, "I am here because of Christian activities, but charged with hooliganism," he could be accused of denigrating the country. The punishment for denigrating the country was very severe.

"What are you here for?" a fellow prisoner asked Costică.

"For criminal behavior," he answered.

"You—a criminal? Come on! Tell me the truth."

Another prisoner asked, "What did you do to be put here?"

"I tried to kill a policeman," he said.

"You tried to kill a policeman? You never tried to kill a chicken."

There was a boy in Costică's dormitory who was due to be released in a few days. One morning he became so weak that he could not get out of bed to go to work. The guards beat him until he fell unconscious. Then they threw him on the cement floor of a "solitary" cell.

Solitary confinement meant that the prisoner had to change into "imitation clothes." This mockery of a uniform was a shirt without a back, trousers with only one leg, and sandals with no soles. Then he had to stand up without a break from five o'clock in the morning till ten o'clock at night on the cold cement floor in complete darkness. The floor was the only toilet and food was served every other day. The guards checked often and unexpectedly to make sure the prisoner did not sit down. Few men risked sitting in the "solitary" cell. The next morning the boy was found dead.

Costică understood better than ever before how Jesus had suffered at the hands of cruel men, and he came to appreciate His suffering in a new way.

As soon as I received my American passport, I booked a ticket to Austria. Stephen met me at the Vienna airport and took me to the mission house.

On August 17, 1985 I went with Stephen to a restaurant to celebrate our engagement. The waiter brought us Wiener schnitzel and salad and sparkling cider. A little live orchestra with a violin and an accordion played for us.

As we ate and drank, Stephen told me what had happened with his team that summer while I was in the States. I knew he was responsible for sending out teams with Bibles. He had to be careful who he sent and where he sent them.

A young man from England had joined the team of Bible smugglers. His name was Joel and he was about eighteen.

He came to Stephen and said, "Please send me to Romania with Bibles. I prayed about it a lot and I would love to go."

"We cannot send any more vehicles with Bibles," Stephen told him. "The Romanians discovered all the systems we used. So if you want to go, it has to be by train."

"That's fine with me," he said.

"I warn you, Joel," Stephen continued, "that they will search your suitcases. You have to be prepared for the worst."

"I know it is dangerous," Joel said, "but I still want to go."

Finally Stephen decided to let him go and bought him a train ticket. He gave him about a hundred small Romanian Bibles. Joel wrapped them with care in sleeping bags and filled his two suitcases with them.

The morning of Joel's departure came. The team prayed for his trip at the morning devotions. Stephen was to drive him to the train station in the city, but somehow they were late leaving the office. The train was due to depart at one o'clock.

"Lord, please delay the train for us," Stephen prayed with Joel as he drove.

To make matters worse, the roads into the city were congested, and the traffic was slow that day.

"Lord, please hold the train up today," Joel prayed too.

"We need a miracle to make it in time," Stephen said.

When they finally arrived at the Südbahnhof, it was bustling with people. Stephen carried one heavy suitcase and Joel carried the other one. They half ran, half stumbled into the station. As they got to the platform, Stephen could hardly believe his eyes—the train was still there. The loud-speakers announced, "The Orient Express is due to depart in two minutes."

Stephen helped Joel onto the train with his two heavy suitcases. He put them on the luggage rack in his compartment. Stephen jumped off just in time.

Joel opened the window and waved good-bye as the train pulled out of the station.

Stephen drove back to the mission house, giving thanks to the Lord. He shared with the team what happened.

He saw the miracle with the train being delayed, but he still wondered how it would turn out for Joel. Boarding a train for Romania did not mean that he would cross the border safely and deliver the Bibles.

Two days later he received a call in his office.

"I'm at the Südbahnhof," came Joel's voice. "Everything went fine."

"Praise the Lord! I'll be right there to pick you up."

He jumped in the car and drove as fast as he could to the station. Joel was in front of the entrance waiting for him.

On the way back to the mission house he told Stephen, "There were eight passengers in my compartment and each of them had at least one suitcase. When we arrived at the Romanian border, the guards checked our passports. Then they checked all the suitcases except mine! I delivered the Bibles to the address in Bucharest you gave me. Then I came back on the next train."

"Praise the Lord!" Stephen said.

That evening the whole team rejoiced.

As Stephen finished his story, we finished our engagement meal in the Viennese restaurant.

"What an incredible story. Thank you for sharing it with me," I said. "It encourages me to trust the Lord for a miracle for my family."

Chapter Ten

The Train of Death

It was late August 1985 and I was now with Stephen in Bexhill-on-Sea, East Sussex, England. We stayed with his parents in their bungalow. Their prayers and encouragement blessed me. I had already met two of his sisters, Ruth and Mary, and now I met his other sister, Olive, with her husband, Geoff, and their baby, Daniel.

I loved the roses in the garden and the cedar tree that spread its branches over the lawn at the back of the house. I enjoyed the delicious cherry tomatoes from the greenhouse. In the evening, I watched with Stephen as a family of hedgehogs came out to drink the milk we left for them on the patio. Yet Costică was in prison for being caught with Bibles in Romania, and I carried a heavy burden on my heart for him wherever I went.

One day I went for a walk with Stephen by the sea, and we sat down on a wooden bench. There we watched the seagulls and talked about our wedding.

"How sad that Costică cannot rejoice with us," I said. "He doesn't even know I get married."

I remembered Costică and Estera's wedding, and suddenly another memory jolted me. I turned to Stephen.

"When I lived in Iași I knew an older lady at the Baptist Church, Elena Boca. She prayed for me, that the Lord would give me a husband."

Stephen squeezed my hand in encouragement, and I shared the story of Elena's vision.

When Costică married Estera in 1978, I prepared a few special songs for the children's choir to sing at the wedding. Elena brought the wedding bench and set it in front of the church. She covered it with a soft wool carpet and helped me make an arch of red roses over the top.

That Sunday afternoon we practiced hard for the occasion. The girls in the choir came to the church dressed in mauve and pink blouses. The boys wore blue shirts and navy trousers.

Costică and Estera entered the church at five o'clock. The hall was packed. Estera was dressed in a long white wedding gown. She wore her hair up with a crown of flowers and a veil. Costică wore a brown suit with a carnation in his lapel. His brown curly hair was combed over his ears. The whole church looked at them and murmurs came from the crowd, "How well they go together! What a beautiful bride Estera is!" Hand in hand, they walked slowly through the crowd toward the front and sat down on the wedding bench.

At that moment I motioned for the children to stand up. They sang the wedding songs I had taught them. My brother Teodor played the organ, Silvia and Nelu played guitars, and my father the violin. I led the children's choir.

Elena's eyes were on Estera and Costică. *How beautiful they look!* she thought. At that moment she had a vision.…

Costică disappeared from the wedding bench, and Estera sat down in the congregation. She was all by herself and dressed in everyday clothes. Elena looked again at the wedding bench. Instead of them, she saw me appear as a bride with a groom she did not know—a young man of medium height, with dark hair combed to one side and a beard.

"The vision lasted long enough to make a strong impression on her mind. Then it disappeared, and she again saw Costică and Estera as the wedding couple."

"How amazing!" Stephen said. "When did Elena tell you the vision?"

"At the wedding meal, in the garden of my parents' house," I answered. "Estera's relatives and my parents prepared everything. About two hundred guests came to the reception, and they sat at long tables under the trees." I nestled against my fiancé, recalling that joyful day. "The first course was chicken borscht with parsley, followed by vine leaves stuffed with rice, ground meat, and vegetables. For dessert there was sweet bread filled with nuts and Turkish delight. There was cool spring water to drink.

"At the meal Elena sat next to me and told me the vision. 'The Lord has a husband for you,' she said."

"It happened exactly like that," Stephen commented. "Now Costică has disappeared in prison…and we are getting married."

I looked at Stephen. He was of medium height, with dark hair and a beard, just as Elena saw in her vision.

As we walked back to the bungalow I prayed for Costică, "Lord, please give him grace and favor and may he know that You are with him."

"And may he be released from there soon," Stephen prayed. "Lord, You came to set the captives free!"

On September 5, 1985, early in the morning, a guard came to Costică in prison.

"We received orders to transfer you to Bucharest," he said.

The guard moved him to a different cell for preparations to be made. From his new cell Costică looked out the window. He recognized the branches a few houses away. It was the cherry tree that he climbed as a child in front of his family home.

It was a windy, rainy morning. Costică followed the guard to an exit door. A police van waited for him and other prisoners. The guards inspected each of them. Some were put in chains before Costică's eyes.

Lord, help me! he prayed.

It was Costică's turn. He watched as the officer looked at his file…then at him…then back at the file. The officer took a pair of chains. Costică prepared his hands and feet to be chained. A sweat passed all over him.

The next moment the officer looked at him again, put the chains down, and pushed him into the van with the other prisoners.

Thank You, Lord, that he did not chain me.

As soon as the door of the van closed, Costică found himself in darkness, as in a closed box. The driver started the engine and drove along bumpy roads. After about twenty minutes, the driver stopped the van and opened the doors.

"Out!" a policeman ordered.

The prisoners got out of the van. Costică looked around and recognized Iaşi's railway station. Escorted by armed police, they crossed over the rails. A freight train waited for them.

"Everyone get on this train," the guards ordered.

Costică climbed onto a wagon that looked like a cattle pen. From there he could not see anything outside and found himself with the other prisoners, again in darkness. Metal bars covered the window, and no fresh air came in.

Suddenly he smelled the coal from the locomotive. The train jolted, starting its journey. It was a seven-hour trip by train from Iaşi to Bucharest. But he did not know that this time it would take much longer....

The train went all over the country and in each place picked up more prisoners. The number in Costică's cage finally reached as many as sixty. Squashed together, tired and hungry, they gasped for air.

A whole day and night passed. From time to time Costică heard a dripping sound. In desperation he stretched out his hands for water...but there was no water. The prisoners were exhausted and standing up without sleep became unbearable. But there was no room to lie down.

After three days and two nights of traveling like this, the train pulled in to the Gara de Nord in Bucharest. The prisoners stumbled out of the train, faint with hunger and thirst. A van waited for them. After half an hour's drive, Rahova Prison opened its gates for them.

The guards led them into a cold room that resembled a mortuary. It was called the Wailing Hall. It had a cement floor and marble benches.

Many prisoners had cried and wailed there. Now it was Costică's turn. Eventually, he lay down on a cold marble bench and fell asleep, but the sleep didn't last long. He was constantly waking up, his feet blue from the cold marble. He rubbed his feet in desperation. They were numb. He fell asleep again, then he woke up with twinges of pain all over. It became a vicious circle for him and the other prisoners for that night and the next day.

If I don't rub my feet, I will die of cold, he thought. *And then what will happen to the children and Estera?* For them he mustered the strength to survive and rubbed his feet again and again.

Then on the second day, the door of the mortuary opened. Officers called the prisoners by name and took them to their respective cells.

"Sfatcu Constantin," the prison officer called.

"Here."

"You? It is written in your file that you should wear chains. Where are your chains?"

Costică kept quiet and in his heart he said, *Thank You, Lord that You saved me from chains.*

"Take all your clothes off and leave them here," the officer shouted. "Go through there." He pointed to a door.

Costică left his clothes and, naked and shivering, walked into another room.

"Body search," a guard ordered.

Costică thought, *Naked I came from my mother's womb, and naked I will depart*, as Job said. *I will not take any riches with me…only what I did for the Lord will count.*

After the guard inspected his clothes, he received them back and put them on. The guard took him to his cell. It was in one of the most secure sections of the prison. He was classified as a person "dangerous for the security of the state."

———————

Though I did not know what went on with Costică in prison, my spirit was continually heavy. All the time I needed to be encouraged by those around me.

One day I had tea with Stephen at his parents' home in Bexhill. We sat down at a table in the garden.

"I want to tell you a story that happened to me four years ago when I traveled to Romania with Bibles," Stephen said.

"Tell me, Stephen. I like to hear stories," I said as I poured the tea. I clung to every word, and my heart cried out for my brother's suffering.

On a summer morning in 1981, Stephen set out from his mission base in Vienna with Colin from Northern Ireland and Ingrid from Finland. Their destination was the town of Arad in western Romania. They had about 1,600 Bibles hidden in the secret compartments of their blue camper van. As usual each of them memorized the address for delivery. The van had only two seats in the front, so they took turns traveling in the back.

They drove and drove all that day until evening. As they traveled Stephen prayed, "Lord, help us to get the Bibles through the border and to deliver them safely."

After they crossed through Hungary, they arrived at the Romanian border. The guards checked their passports, gave the van a quick search, and waved them through without any problem.

Wonderful! Stephen thought as they entered Romania. *Will the whole trip be that easy?*

At ten o'clock the next night they parked the van in a safe unloading place. They finished their late supper, a bottle of fruit yogurt and nuts. Now they were ready for work. Ingrid got out to keep watch in the moonlight.

Colin and Stephen got in the back of the van. They drew the curtains and opened the secret compartments. It took them a good hour of hard work to put the Bibles into plastic sacks ready for delivery. When they finished, Colin got back into the driver's seat and Ingrid got in beside him. Stephen remained in the back and sat on a sack of Bibles.

Colin drove along the bumpy back streets of Arad toward their contact's house. From the back, Stephen tried to see the road ahead through a small gap in the curtains.

Suddenly Colin shouted, "Police! Stephen, don't move. Keep quiet."

Stephen quickly lay down on top of the sacks of Bibles between the benches in the back of the van.

The officer signaled Colin to stop. He pulled the van to the side of the road, turned off the engine, and lowered the window.

Lord, don't let them open the back, Stephen prayed. *Please save us and the Bibles.*

"*Actele la control*," the police officer said.

Colin and Ingrid handed him their passports and the vehicle papers for inspection.

If he opens the back door, we are finished, Stephen thought. *Help, Lord!*

The officer checked the vehicle papers. He then looked at Colin's passport in his hand. In the light of his flashlight he looked back and forth from the passport picture to Colin's face. Then he did the same with Ingrid's passport. It seemed to take forever.

"Are there just the two of you?" the policeman asked in English.

Colin looked at Ingrid, then back at the officer. He put up two fingers.

The police officer laughed.

"Have a good trip," he said and handed back the papers.

How happy Stephen was when he heard the engine start again and felt the van move!

After half and hour of driving they arrived at the contact's house, delivered the Bibles, and headed for the border rejoicing.

I had listened to Stephen's story spellbound. "Thank you, Stephen, for that wonderful story. It encourages me to trust the Lord for my family."

Lord, I cast my care upon You, I prayed. *You will take care of Costică and the rest of my family.*

Genovieva meets Costică, Estera, Teo, and Genovieva
at Rome airport, July 1986

Genovieva with Costică, Estera, Teo, and Genovieva
at Rome airport, July 1986

Chapter Eleven

The Appeal

It was now late September 1985. My brother Costică was still in Rahova Prison in Bucharest. His official crime was trying to kill the officer who stopped him. My family told me on the phone that they made an appeal against his sentence. *What will result from it?* I wondered. *Will they set him free or will something worse happen to him?*

I was in England with Stephen, preparing for our wedding. We stayed with Stephen and Joanne Hall, friends of ours in Guildford. One warm, sunny afternoon we sat in their garden. We admired the blue and purple Michaelmas daisies with their golden centers.

Coo, coo, coo…coo, coo. We heard the wood pigeons in the fir tree as we ate our wheat rolls with cheese and tomatoes. A squirrel ran across the soft green lawn and joined us.

It was lovely to be with Stephen, but from time to time I sank into sadness, and he noticed.

He opened the Bible and read from Psalm 103:6, "'The LORD works righteousness and justice for all the oppressed.' Let's not forget what the Lord did in the past, Genovieva," he said as he drank his tea. "I remember when I was a Bible smuggler.…"

"Another story? Tell me. Your stories always encourage me."

"Well, I knew the believers in East Germany did not have Christian literature and I wanted to help them. I transported literature many times along the transit routes."

"What do you mean by transit routes?" I asked.

Stephen explained the historical background. After Germany's defeat in World War II, the country was divided into East and West. The capital, Berlin, was also divided into sectors. The Russian sector became East Berlin, which was also the capital of the German Democratic Republic. The American, British, and French sectors of the city became West Berlin. In order for the residents of West Berlin to travel to West Germany, several transit routes were designated between West Berlin and West Germany. Travelers could pass freely through East Germany on these transit routes.

Traveling on the transit routes was simple as long as you obeyed the rules. It was forbidden to leave the transit route, and you were expected to arrive at the other end within five hours. Vehicles traveling to West Berlin were not inspected at the borders of the German Democratic Republic, and that provided a window of opportunity for missions helping the East German Christians.

On one occasion, Stephen traveled with a Canadian friend, Victor. At the East German border, after they paid the transit visa fee, the guards checked their passports and stamped them with the date and time.

Their mission had many contacts in East Germany who lived near the transit routes. They were always glad to receive and distribute Christian literature.

For this work, it was essential to drive by night. They timed their journey so that they would arrive at their contact's house about midnight. Then they would quickly get off the transit route at the nearest exit, drive straight to their contact, and unload the van. They had a cup of coffee and prayer with the family, then headed back to the transit route. They usually made it to West Berlin well within the time limit. The East German guards never knew that they had left the transit route.

But this time things were different. Their contact lived fifty miles off the transit route. They drove to his house with no problem and dropped the load. But when they headed back, Stephen missed an exit and they got lost. Then at a check point the police stopped them. An officer took their passports and looked at the visas.

"I see that you have transit, not tourist visas," he said. "Don't you know that it is forbidden to leave the transit route?"

"Sorry," Stephen said. "I took a wrong turn somewhere."

The officer walked around the van and looked in the back.

Thank God we delivered the load! Stephen thought.

The officer returned their passports and directed them back to the transit route. When they arrived at the control post at the other end, the communist guards ordered them to drive the van into a garage for an inspection. They went through all their personal things and searched their wallets very thoroughly.

"Do you know anyone in the German Democratic Republic?"

"No," Stephen said. *After all, I only exchanged a few words with the contact*, he thought.

After they paid a fine, the guards let them go. How much Stephen rejoiced that they accomplished their mission!

The next time his friend Victor went to East Germany, though, the police caught him on his way to the contact. They confiscated everything: the literature and the vehicle. They arrested him and his friend Randy and interrogated them for three days in East Berlin.

"It is amazing how many times you escaped, Stephen," I said. "The Lord delivered you again and again. His hand of favor was upon you in a special way."

Will His hand of favor be upon Costică too? I wondered.

The discipline in Rahova Prison in Romania where Costică was held for Bibles was severe. Any sign of resistance was paid back with beatings.

"Clean every inch of the cell," the guard shouted to Costică and the other prisoners.

"I want those bars to shine," another guard ordered.

Costică got down on his knees every day and cleaned every inch of the cell with a cloth.

"I am very sick and I can't hear," he told a guard one day.

"Okay, I will report it," he said.

A week passed and no doctor or medicine came.

"I have an ear infection and a fever," he told another guard. But the guard just shrugged.

I can't hear the sound of the chains of my fellow prisoners...nor the loud knocks on the door of the cell in the morning, he thought. *Will I be deaf for the rest of my life?*

In such a state, on September 26, 1985, Costică was taken from his cell, handcuffed, and driven off in a prison van.

Where do they take me? he wondered.

The van stopped outside a large brick building with many cars parked in front. He recognized it to be the courthouse in Bucharest. *My family appealed my sentence,* he thought.

Costică was taken inside and led into the dock. Trembling, he took a quick look into the audience. The large hall was packed. On his right he saw his wife, mother, brothers, and sister. They smiled at him and waved. He noticed some important-looking people seated around his family. They were well dressed and looked like foreigners. He felt they were on his side.

These friends, who came especially for the appeal, were United States Representatives Tony Hall, Chris Smith, Frank Wolf, and Mark Siljander; State Representative Tom Riner; State Senator Gene Huff; and David Atkinson and Thomas Clarke, Members of the British Parliament.

A gong sounded. The crowd became quiet.

The chief prosecutor stood up and read a typed statement.

"We agree to reconsider the case of Sfatcu Constantin," he started. "He is accused of the attempted murder of a police officer...."

He went on for a few minutes then he sat down.

"Where are the plaintiff and the prosecution witness?" the judge asked.

"Your honor, the plaintiff and the witness send their apologies," a clerk stood up and explained. "They could not attend for personal reasons."

Then it was the turn of the defense attorney.

"Your honor, I bring to your attention that the plaintiff and the prosecution witness changed their original declarations."

He proceeded to read their revised declarations to the court.

Costică watched everything, but he could not hear. He tried to read lips.

"Do you have anything to say in your defense?" the judge asked him.

"I am not guilty!" Costică said, and tears ran down his cheeks.

The gong sounded again.

"The session is over," the clerk said. "The judge will announce his decision later."

The crowd disbursed. The foreign officials invited my family out for a meal. Everyone in my family felt so loved and blessed by them.

After the appeal, Costică was taken back to prison. *Is there any hope for me, Lord? Will I ever be free again?* he wondered. *No one even told me my sentence.*

One day a fellow prisoner asked him, "What is your sentence?"

"I don't know," Costică answered.

"Then…you must be sentenced to death like the rest of us."

"We are all on death row in this cell," another inmate said.

Cold shivers went through Costică's body. His heart beat fast. *Lord, help me to die faithful to You.*

The only way the guards spoke to Costică was through signs. He was considered a dangerous enemy of the state.

One day a few weeks later, an officer came and made signs to him. Costică understood and followed him into the prison yard. He wore his thin prison clothes and tennis shoes. The officer motioned to him to go down into a hole. The hole had bars over the top. He sat down on the ground at the bottom. It started to snow, and soon snowflakes covered his head. He shivered there from the cold.

After a few hours, the same officer came back. He made signs to him. Costică followed him back to the cell.

That evening for supper they ate boiled corn and cabbage soup. Costică looked at the faces of the other prisoners. *O, Lord, how skinny and pale they are!* he thought. *And I must look the same.*

The days in prison passed very slowly. From five o'clock in the morning till half past ten at night, the guards forbade them to lie down on the beds. They walked only a few feet up and down the room.

Another time a fellow prisoner started to beat Costică.

"Help! Help! He is killing me!" Costică screamed, but no one came to his rescue.

When his assailant got tired, he rested for a while then started again to hit him unmercifully with his fists and kick him all over. Costică put his hands around his head to protect himself. He did not fight back.

"Help me, God!" he cried. "Save me, O God!"

The next day, when the assailant seemed calm, Costică asked him, "Why did you do that to me?"

"The director promised me an early release if I could make you hit me back," he said.

A week later a man in a suit came into his cell.

"Hello, Mr. Sfatcu," the man said. "I work for the government. I came to make you an offer. If you cooperate, you can go home today."

"What is the offer?" Costică asked.

"Just tell us how Bibles get into the country and who distributes them."

"I already told you all I know. I have nothing more to say."

"Then you will spend a long time here," the man said and left.

It was a cold winter and the food was so poor. At night Costică sat hunched up under his blanket. He put his arms around his legs to warm up. He knew he was only skin and bones. A verse from the Bible came to his mind: "This poor man called, and the LORD heard him; he saved him out of all his troubles" (Psalm 34:6).

———————————

A week later Estera received a letter from the judge. It stated that Costică's sentence was reduced from seven and a half years to four and a half years. But the secret police made it impossible for anyone to send this news to Costică.

Chapter Twelve

A Parcel Returned

After the appeal in Bucharest, no one told Costică the outcome. He continued to believe that his sentence was death or life in prison. "Even if kings and queens come, no one can save the Sfatcus from our hands!" the commander of the secret police threatened.

At this time I was with Stephen in Guildford, England. We stayed with our friends in their lovely five-bedroom house. The flowers in the windows and the oak furniture with large mirrors gave the house its charm. It was a cold day and I wore my red woolen suit; Stephen wore a blue sweater knitted by his mother. We sat by the fireplace in the living room and drank a cup of hot cider with cinnamon.

Stephen had a part-time job at Keston College, a center for the study of religion and communism. He also took care of most of the preparations for the wedding. That afternoon I helped him send out the invitations. The grandfather clock in the corner kept us company with its chimes: *Ding-dong-ding-dong!*

"Why can't we have a normal wedding, full of joy, like any other couple?" I asked Stephen. "Costică is in prison and they try to arrest Teodor and Erzso as well."

"The Lord will bless those who suffer for Him," Stephen replied. "Let me tell you a story that happened to me." Strangely, I thought, his eyes sparkled with humor.

Many believers behind the Iron Curtain risked their lives for the Bible. In Siberia Bibles were very scarce. The only way for the Christians there to have Bibles was to print them on underground printing presses. Families lived underground for years in order to print Bibles, which others then distributed. Printing presses were smuggled into Russia in parts and assembled there underground. The presses continually needed supplies of ink and sometimes replacement parts from the West.

Stephen helped to send couriers to Moscow or Leningrad for this cause. He also went himself as a courier to take ink. It was the spring of 1982. His friend Dave from England accompanied him. In the office of their mission house in Vienna, they worked hard to prepare for the trip. They made special thick, strong plastic bags for the ink. The bags measured two feet long by six inches wide. Each held two liters of ink. Stephen placed one bag over each of his shoulders and taped them to his skin. He then secured a third bag around his waist, using a long, cloth bandage and safety pins. Dave did the same. The twelve liters of ink they carried between them would print a few thousand Bibles in Siberia.

In order to travel without arousing suspicion they had to wear thick clothes. Stephen wore a vest, a thick shirt, a sweater, and corduroy trousers. He packed a change of clothes in his suitcase. The team prayed for them and they left.

They boarded the train in Vienna in the afternoon. It traveled through Hungary toward the Soviet Union. Fortunately, there was no one else in their compartment. They made themselves comfortable for the twelve-hour journey to Kiev. Soon the Hungarian customs officers came through. They inspected their visas and looked in their suitcases. Then Stephen made his seat into a bed and lay down. *How wonderful that I can rest,* he thought. But his rest was to be short.

Suddenly he felt something wet at his back. *Oh, no. Surely not.*

He got up, walked along the corridor to the restroom, and locked himself in.

The train sped on its way. *Clickety-click, clickety-click*, he heard from under his feet. He leaned against the back of the door to keep his balance and looked under his shirt. *Where exactly is the leak?* His heart beat fast. The ink had leaked from one of the bags over his shoulders, down his back into his shirt and trousers. He removed the tape that kept the bag in place and threw it and the bag down the toilet onto the tracks. He saw the gleam of a rail and the blur of sleepers through the hole.

He cautiously opened the door…looked right and left. *No one around.* He ran back to the compartment.

"Dave, quick! Bring me a change of clothes in the restroom…everything!"

He dashed back to the restroom. *Thank You, Lord, that no one occupied it*, he prayed as he locked himself in again.

A few minutes later Dave came with the clothes. Stephen took them and locked the door again.

He knew he would be there for some time. *I have to be organized*, he thought. *Help me, Lord!* He hung the clean clothes safely on a hook, then took off his shirt, vest, and trousers. Down the toilet they went. His hands were black, his waist was black, and when he pulled off his vest, he even got ink in his hair. Then he started to clean himself up with soap and water. He looked in the mirror to see if he was clean. Stubborn traces of ink remained.

Someone tried the door. He heard two ladies talking. "Let's wait a little until the bathroom is free," one of them said.

You will have to wait a long, long time! Stephen thought. He was relieved when he heard them go away. *What if the border guards come and order me out?* He knew that they could inspect the restrooms at any time. Horror filled his heart.

He looked around and saw ink everywhere—in the sink, on the walls and on the floor. He used up all the paper towels and toilet tissues to clean it up. He did not want to leave anything suspicious behind him.

The whole operation took several hours. When everything was clean, he put on his new clothes and emerged a new man.

Thank You, Lord that You saved me, he prayed.

The next night they delivered ten liters of ink to their contact in Kiev. He took it further to the underground Bible printing presses in Siberia.

I laughed a lot listening to Stephen's story.

―――――――――――

On November 16, 1985 I married Stephen in the Baptist Church in Guildford, Surrey, England. I wore a long white gown with flowers in my crown, and a veil. Stephen wore a light brown herringbone suit with a white carnation in his lapel. Gene Huff kept his promise and came to give me away. His wife, Ethel, and another couple accompanied him. Two of Stephen's sisters, Ruth and Mary, were my bridesmaids. They wore pale turquoise dresses with floral patterns. Paul Booth, who had come to Romania with Stephen on his first visit, was the best man.

About a hundred people attended the service, and the church helped us with the reception. To my surprise, my mother received a passport at the last minute and attended the wedding. Silvia and Elena, my long time friends from Romania, also came from the United States. Stephen and Joanne Hall helped to put up some of the guests who needed overnight accommodation. Stephen's parents came from Bexhill and stayed with them.

While we went into a back room to sign the marriage register, a cassette recording of my children's choir from Romania was played.

The reception was held in the church hall. The guests helped themselves to all sorts of delicacies on long tables: Romanian stuffed cabbage, grilled chicken, roast beef, wild rice with herbs, salads, cheeses, fruits, and all sorts of desserts and cakes. The wedding cake was a fruit cake with icing. There was a lemon meringue pie among others for dessert.

Senator Gene Huff sat on my right, and my mother sat next to him. Gene said to me, "This meringue pie is delicious. Everyone goes for seconds. I will get myself another serving before it runs out," he said as he stood up.

He came back with a second portion and set it down at his place. But before he sat down to eat it he turned around to speak for a minute to the best man. Meanwhile, my mother thought the pie was for her. She pulled it toward her. When Senator Huff sat down, it was almost all gone.

"You stole my pie!" he told her.

My mother giggled with laughter for the rest of the reception. I was glad to see her happy for a change.

———————

As a wedding present to us, Gene and Ethel Huff and their friends traveled on to Romania to see my family. We gave them some dry salami to take to my family for Costică. When they arrived in Bucharest they took a taxi to Rahova Prison.

As they arrived at the gate, Gene pulled out his identification and showed it to the guard on duty.

"I am Senator Gene Huff from Kentucky," he said.

"What do you want?" the guard asked.

"I came to see Constantin Sfatcu."

"Only his family is allowed to visit him," the guard replied.

"I am his brother," Gene responded.

The guard talked on the phone. He made them wait for about an hour.

"You are not allowed to see him," the guard said finally. "Please leave immediately."

From Bucharest Senator Huff and his party went to Iaşi. They visited my family and the church and their visit encouraged everyone so much.

While Costică was in prison, Estera's boss told her to divorce him. He said that no one wanted to work with a prisoner's wife. When she refused, he pressured her to resign. Estera refused to sign the paper of resignation, presented to her several times. *Lord, don't let me lose my job*, she prayed. *I would lose my income and my ration card for food.*

Estera was afraid to leave the children by themselves, even for a minute. She feared the police might kidnap them. Her mother stayed with them while she was at work. Children of prisoners were often stopped in the street on their way home from school and beaten by the secret police.

Teo was six and Genovieva was five at the time. They prayed every day, "Lord, keep Dad well in prison; keep him warm, and don't let him go hungry."

The secret police watched Estera's house day and night. Estera's mother always slept with them. One night at about two o'clock, they heard a noise on the roof. It sounded as if two or three men climbed into the attic and walked around. *Creak-creak. Crack-crack.* Everyone woke up and listened. Terror struck Estera and the children.

"Let's get out of the house," Estera said.

They all ran outside into the yard. Suddenly Teo was not afraid anymore. He looked up at the roof, put his hands around his mouth, and shouted as loud as he could, "Policemen, get down from the roof! Otherwise I will call the Americans!"

The men left soon after that, and the family went back to bed.

In December Estera received a card from Rahova Prison. It informed her that she could visit her husband and take him a five-kilo food parcel.

"We can go and see Dad!" she told the children.

"When can we go? When can we go?" they asked and jumped up and down with excitement.

"Let's get ready now," she said.

The children helped their mother to make the food parcel. They put in it dry cheese, dry salami, nuts, and cookies.

That night Estera and the children took a train to Bucharest. Teo and Genovieva fell asleep on her lap. All the way she dreamed of the moment when they would be together with Costică. She prepared in her mind words of love and encouragement for him.

The train pulled in at the Gara de Nord at six o'clock the next morning. A taxi took them to the prison. They arrived at the gate cold and tired. Estera handed the officer on duty the card with her husband's name on it. He took it and checked the name on a list.

"Sfatcu Constantin is no longer here," he said.

"Where is he then?" Estera asked.

"Look for him in Iaşi," the guard suggested.

"Please check again," she asked.

The guard called the director.

"No, he is not here," he said and returned the card.

Estera and the children left the prison with tears in their eyes. They cried all the way back to the railway station. Then they set off on the two-hundred-and-fifty-mile train journey back to Iaşi.

When she arrived home, Estera found a parcel.

"The postman brought it this morning," her mother said.

Estera quickly opened it.

"Costică's clothes...returned from the prison in Bucharest!" She looked for a note of explanation, but found none.

"He must be dead," she said and started to cry again.

Her mother hugged her.

The next day she remembered what the guard in Bucharest told her. She went to the prison in Iaşi and asked if Costică was there. But no one seemed to know his whereabouts. For the next two months, she went from prison to prison looking for her husband, dead or alive.

There is no hope. He must be dead, she finally thought.

One evening Estera's uncle Avram came from Rădăuți to visit her and the children.

"Let me tell you a dream the Lord gave me," he began. "In my dream I saw seven judges at a long table. They were all dressed in black robes with black hoods. Costică stood in front of them. He was dressed in white. The rest of the family stood at the door trembling. The seven judges pointed their fingers at them, bringing accusations.

"Then suddenly a mighty wind came through the door and windows into the room. The wind was so strong that it blew off the black hoods…the black robes…and then struck to the ground the seven judges. And Costică and the family broke free!"

"Thank you, uncle Avram," Estera said.

O Lord, may it come true soon!

Genovieva with Costică, Estera, Teo, and Genovieva
outside Pensione Etnea, Rome, where they stayed for ten days
before their departure for the United States, July 1986

Genovieva meets Teodor and Erzso at Rome airport,
September 1986

Chapter Thirteen

Costică's Dream

After our wedding we rented a house in the village of Shalford, near Guildford. Stephen continued to work at Keston College and kept them informed about my family. Many missions took their information about the suffering church from Keston's news service. Costică's case received worldwide publicity. To raise support for my family, I took every opportunity to speak about the situation in Romania. I spoke in churches, schools, and women's groups and gave radio and television interviews.

Christian Solidarity International invited me to speak about my family at a reception in the House of Commons. While at the House of Commons, I also gave an interview to a Romanian reporter with Radio Free Europe. The interview was broadcast into Romania several times. President Ronald Reagan mentioned the Sfatcu family in the United States Congress and demanded their release as a condition for the renewal of most-favored nation status for Romania. Secretary of State Shultz met personally with Ceauşescu regarding their case. In spite of all our efforts and publicity, nothing changed for my family.

In March 1986 I started an intensive, three-month radio training course with Radio Worldwide in Bexhill-on-Sea. They trained missionaries from around the world to broadcast the gospel to their own people. The chief examiner came from the BBC.

After Senator Huff visited the prison, everyone in Costică's cell received an extra blanket and double portions of food.

One night Costică had a dream. The next morning he shared it with the other prisoners. "In my dream I saw a young fir tree with many green branches," he started. "Then I saw a hand. The hand reached to the tree and broke off a little branch. The dream was vivid and clear."

The inmates listened attentively. One of them, a young gypsy, said, "This is the interpretation of your dream: The young fir tree is you. The many green branches are many good years ahead for you. The hand that reached to the tree and broke off a little branch means that you will be in prison only for one year. Then you will be free."

"How I wish it would be so," Costică said.

After many weeks of searching, Estera found Costică in Rahova Prison in Bucharest. He had been there all the time. She was allowed to visit her husband in prison once every five months for ten minutes.

Estera and the children arrived at the prison and went to the meeting point. They talked to Costică under the watchful eye of an armed guard.

He is so skinny, Estera thought as she looked at her husband, *and what awful clothes he is wearing! But I love him so much.*

"I miss you, Estera," Costică said with tears in his eyes.

During the visit, little Teo went up to the guard, pulled his sleeve, and asked, "Uncle, when will you let Dad come home?"

The guard shuffled his feet in embarrassment.

The visit was short, but Estera was happy. *Thank You, Lord, that You kept Costică alive*, she prayed. *When will he be free?*

On April 18, 1986 a guard moved Costică to another cell and left him there alone. Rivers of joy filled his heart. He remembered a song and sang it over and over again.

> "Christ is risen from the dead!
> By His death He overcame death.
> Now to the dead He gives Life!"

Costică prayed, *Thank You, Lord, that You are my Savior. You are my greatest joy!*

On April 19, 1986, exactly one year after his arrest, two officers came and told him, "We received orders to release you from prison. You can go home today!"

That morning Estera received a call at work.

"I have good news for you," the pastor's wife said. "Constantin is free! He is coming home by train this evening."

Estera shouted for joy! She went home and took all the money she had in the house. She ran to the market and found an old man with a bucket of flowers waiting for customers.

"Sell me all the flowers my money can buy," she said. "Here are two hundred *lei*. This is a great day in my life. My husband is free and will be home tonight!"

The old man became happy too and said, "Take all the flowers in the bucket."

With her arms full of flowers she ran home. She laughed and shouted aloud, "He is free! He is free! He is coming home!"

She did not care that people stared at her. Exactly one year before, she had wept aloud as she walked that same street on her way back from the police station. Now was the time to rejoice aloud.

That evening Costică arrived home. The news of his release went around fast. Their house was once again filled with brothers and sisters from the church who came to rejoice with them. Even non-Christian neighbors came and said, "Your God is the only true God!"

One morning I was attending classes at the radio training course at Hurchington Manor, Bexhill-on-Sea, England. The phone rang.

"It is for you, Genovieva," my teacher, Phil Booth, told me.

"Hello," I said.

"It's me," Stephen said. His voice gave away his excitement. "Costică is free and is at home with Estera!"

"Oh, how wonderful!" I said and jumped up and down for joy.

A great revival happened in Iaşi because of my family's suffering. The church was united in prayer. One evening sixty people visited the church out of curiosity and they were all saved that night. At their baptism, a few months later, another thirty people gave their lives to the Lord.

Soon after Costică's release, all my family received political asylum in the United States. Costică and Estera and their children left Romania in June 1986. They had another son, Stephen, in Whittier, California. Teodor and Erzso left Romania in September 1986 and had a daughter, Joy, and a son, Nathan, in Riverside, California. My mother left Romania in 1987 along with my sister, Aurora, and her husband, Virgil, and their two children, Laura and Babi. Finally, my brother Dionisie and his wife, Virginia, and their children, Corina, Iulian, Vlad, and Bogdan also left Romania and settled in California.

From America we never forgot those who remained behind in Romania. I started a mission with Stephen to reach out to the poor and to spread the gospel in my homeland, especially among children. After the revolution in 1989, we were able to multiply our efforts. For more information, please visit our Web site: www.genovieva.org.